CANADIAN FIREARMS SAFETY COURSE

AIMING FOR SAFETY

Library and Archives Canada Cataloguing in Publication

Canadian Firearms Safety Course: Student Handbook - 4th edition

Also available in French under the title, Cours canadien dans le maniement des armes à feu, manuel de l'étudiant. *(Également disponible en français sous le titre, Cours canadien dans le maniement des armes à feu, manuel de l'étudiant.)*

ISBN 978-0-660-19826-2

Catalogue no.: PS99-2/2-2008E

1. Firearms--Canada--Safety measures.

2. Firearms ownership--Canada.

3. Firearms--Safety measures.

4. Gun control--Canada.

I. Royal Canadian Mounted Police (RCMP) / Canada Firearms Centre (CAFC)

TS532.2.C36 2008   363.330971   C2006-980173-3

This edition of the Canadian Firearms Safety Course is produced by:
Technical Documentation and Graphics Section
Information Management Branch / CIO Sector
RCMP Headquarters
Ottawa ON K1A 0R2 Canada

Fax: 613-825-9617

PREFACE

Acknowledgements

Many organizations with an ongoing interest in firearms safety volunteered their time to review and comment on this Handbook during its developmental stages. The efforts and assistance of the many people involved (see below) are acknowledged and appreciated. Without their help and that of the following organizations, this Handbook would not have been possible:

- Chief Firearms Officers and their Staff

- Central Forensic Laboratory, RCMP

- International Hunter Education Association (IHEA)

- Saskatchewan Association for Firearm Education (SAFE)

- Firearms Safety Education Service of Ontario (FSESO)

- Nova Scotia Hunter & Firearm Safety Education Instructors Association

- National Firearms Association (NFA)

- User Group on Firearms

- Coalition for Gun Control

- Info-sécure Inc.

Most importantly, the RCMP/CAFC wishes to acknowledge the talent and expertise of the certified Instructors of the Canadian Firearms Safety Course from across Canada, many of whom took the time and effort to provide written recommendations and suggestions in the development of this material.

Disclaimer

The improper use of firearms may result in serious injury. The material presented in this Handbook is intended to demonstrate the operation of firearms in accordance with safe handling techniques and an awareness of manufacturers' specifications and safety features.

The RCMP/CAFC makes no warranties whatsoever, either express or implied, oral or written, in fact or by operation of law or otherwise, regarding the safety of any firearm or the use of any safety mechanism shown in the Handbook.

Individuals should use firearms in accordance with manufacturers' specifications and contact individual manufacturers as each model features different safety mechanisms and some of the techniques demonstrated might not be appropriate for certain firearms.

Ultimately, responsibility for firearm safety rests with the individual.

Table of Contents

List of Figures

	Name	Section
1.	Cannon	1.1.0
2.	Matchlock	1.1.1
3.	Wheel lock	1.1.2
4.	Flintlocks	1.1.3
5a.	Flintlock pistol	1.1.3
5b.	Flintlock rifle	1.1.3
6.	Percussion cap on a lock	1.1.7
7.	Examples of modern cartridges	1.1.8
8.	Major firearms parts	1.2.0
9.	Firing sequence	1.3
10.	Types of firearms actions	1.4
11.	Various firearm locking devices	2.3
12.	Rifled versus smooth-bore barrels	3.1
13.	Cross-section view of various chokes and illustration of shotgun patterns (30" patterning target)	3.3
14.	Types of shotgun slugs	3.4
15.	Shotgun gauge (not to scale)	3.5
16.	Ammunition components for a muzzleloader	3.6.2
17.	Example of a rim-fire and centre-fire cartridge with head stamp	3.7.0
18.	Example of a barrel data stamp	3.7.0
19.	Centre-fire bullet, powder charge, case, and primer	3.7.1
20.	Examples of rifle bullets	3.7.1
21.	Rim-fire cartridge	3.7.2
22.	Centre-fire cartridge	3.7.2
23.	Cartridge head stamp, data stamp and ammunition box label	3.7.3

List of Tables

	Name	Section
1.	The Vital Four ACTS of Firearms Safety	Introduction
2.	Evolution of Firearms	1.1.10
3.	The Vital Four ACTS of Firearms Safety	2.1.0
4.	Types of Black Powder	3.6.1
5.	Cartridge Components and Materials	3.7.1
6.	Typical Cartridge Names and Actual Diameters	3.7.4
7.	Ammunition Safety Points to Remember	3.12
8.	The Vital Four ACTS of Firearms Safety	4.5.0
9.	Magazine-Size Limits	4.9.2
10.	Carrying Positions	5.8
11.	Firearm Hazards and Precautions	8.6
12.	Social Responsibilities of a Firearms User (summary of)	8.8
13.	Some Legal Responsibilities of a Firearms User	8.9
14.	Non-Restricted Firearms (classes of firearms)	9.1.1
15.	Restricted Firearms (classes of firearms)	9.1.2
16.	Prohibited Firearms (classes of firearms)	9.1.3
17.	Ammunition	9.2.0
18.	Prohibited Ammunition	9.2.1
19.	Prohibited Devices	9.2.2
20.	The Vital Four ACTS of Firearms Safety	9.7

List of Charts

	Name	Section
1.	Comparison of Rifle Cartridges and Shotgun Shells	3.7.5
2.	Shot Sizes	3.8.2
3.	Dangerous Range of Rifle Ammunition	3.9
4.	Dangerous Range of Shotgun Ammunition	3.9

INTRODUCTION TO THE
CANADIAN FIREARMS
SAFETY COURSE

INTRODUCTION

Introduction to the Course

The Canadian Firearms Safety Course (CFSC) is designed to apply to the broadest possible spectrum of novice firearm users. Existing firearm safety courses across Canada have a proven track record in the reduction of firearm-related incidents. However, most of these courses have been designed and delivered for firearms use in a specific activity. The CFSC is an introductory firearm safety course intended for all new firearms users.

Individuals who wish to acquire restricted firearms must also pass the Canadian Restricted Firearms Safety Course tests.

The Canadian Firearms Program

The Canadian Firearms Program is administered by the RCMP/CAFC, which works with provincial Chief Firearms Officers and many community partners across the country in implementing the *Firearms Act* and its regulations, and other related legislation regarding firearms.

The goal of the Canadian Firearms Program is the safe and responsible use of firearms, and it includes a range of activities directed toward achieving that goal such as the following:

- The **licensing** of all firearm owners and businesses
- The **registration** of all firearms
- The delivery of the **Canadian Firearms Safety Courses**
- **Public education** regarding safe storage, transport and use of firearms, and
- **Import and export controls**

Licensing, registration and other Program information is recorded in the Canadian Firearms Information System, a national database that is managed by the RCMP/CAFC. Certain information is available to law enforcement agencies to help them prevent and investigate firearms incidents and crime, consistent with the public safety objectives of the *Firearms Act.*

Your personal information is carefully protected by the Canadian Firearms Program, consistent with the *Firearms Act* and its *Regulations,* federal and provincial privacy laws and other applicable statutes.

If you have any questions about the Canadian Firearms Program, please contact us at the following location:

RCMP/CAFC	
Telephone:	1-800-731-4000 (toll-free)
Fax:	613-825-0297
Email:	cfc-cafc@cfc-cafc.gc.ca
Address:	Royal Canadian Mounted Police / Canada Firearms Centre Ottawa ON K1A OR2

You can also consult the *Firearms Act* and its *Regulations* directly via the RCMP/CAFC website.

The RCMP/CAFC wishes you the best in following the Canadian Firearms Safety Courses(s) for the class(es) of firearms you wish to acquire and/or possess. Please note that all Canadian Firearm Safety Course instructors and examiners must be certified by the Chief Firearms Officer for the province or territory in which you are taking the course.

Course Objectives

Firearm owners have social responsibilities. By completing this course, you will be instructed on what these responsibilities are. You will learn how to do the following:

- Handle firearms and ammunition safely.

- Use firearms and ammunition safely.

- Comply with firearms laws.

- Store non-restricted firearms and ammunition safely.

- Display non-restricted firearms safely.

- Transport non-restricted firearms safely.

The Canadian Firearms Safety Course consists of two parts. One is classroom instruction. The other is learning the material in this handbook. There will be both written and practical examinations. Passing them will demonstrate the knowledge and skills you have gained in the course. Live firing exercises, however, are not offered as part of this course.

During the course, some topics are discussed and explored several times. This will help you learn and retain the content. Leaving anything out of the course will reduce the amount you learn. This applies to all assignments, exercises or examinations given by your instructor.

The course emphasizes safe storage, display, transportation, handling and use of non-restricted firearms. But safety depends on more than just safe physical actions.

Safe handling must include greater knowledge of the firearms themselves, ammunition, and the laws and regulations related to them.

Course Handbook

Safety also relies on your attitude about responsible handling and use of firearms. Pay close attention to the section on legal, ethical and social responsibilities. The safety of the people around you depends on it. Your own safety depends on it, also.

This book is an essential part of the course. The other parts are the classroom lessons and practical exercises given by the instructor. Together they will help you learn how to safely handle firearms.

This book contains the following elements:

- The **Vital Four ACTS** of firearm safety

- A brief history of firearms

- Information on firearms and ammunition and how they work

- Instructions on how to pick up, handle and carry non-restricted firearms safely

- Descriptions of how to unload, load and fire non-restricted firearms safely

- Descriptions of the correct firing positions

- Instructions on range safety

- Instructions on the care and cleaning of non-restricted firearms

- Examples of factors leading to firearm accidents and the misuse of firearms

- A summary of ethics and laws affecting firearm owners and users

- Information on how to store, display, transport and handle non-restricted firearms safely

- A glossary of firearm terms

- Appendixes

This is an introductory course. More information and training is available on the various shooting sports from their own qualified instructors, associations and local clubs. We recommend you contact them directly for further details.

Also, do not hesitate to contact provincial/territorial or local authorities for more detailed information on firearm laws and regulations in your area.

Consult the *Firearms Act* and *Regulations* or a firearms officer, for information on controls affecting firearm and ammunition manufacturers, dealers and museum operators.

The Vital Four ACTS of Firearm Safety

Your instructor will refer to many different safety rules and guidelines. But time and again, the instructor will return to four basic rules. Any time you hear of an accident occurring, you can be sure at least one of these rules has been broken. These rules are known as the **Vital Four ACTS.**

The first letter of each rule becomes a letter in the acronym **ACTS.** You may want to think of these rules as acts you must carry out.

Table 1. The Vital Four ACTS of Firearm Safety

The Vital Four ACTS of Firearm Safety	
👉	**Assume every firearm is loaded.** • Regard any firearm as a potential danger.
👉	**Control the muzzle direction at all times.** • Identify the safest available muzzle direction. • Keep the firearm pointed in the safest available direction. • The muzzle of a firearm should not be pointed towards yourself or any other person.
👉	**Trigger finger must be kept off the trigger and out of the trigger guard.** • Resist the temptation to put your finger on the trigger or inside the trigger guard when you pick up a firearm. • Accidental discharge is far more likely to occur if your finger is on the trigger or inside the trigger guard.
👉	**See that the firearm is unloaded - PROVE it safe.** • Do not handle the firearm unless you can properly **PROVE** it safely. • Check to see that both chamber and magazine are empty. Do this every time you handle a firearm, for any reason. • Pass or accept only open and unloaded firearms. This is an important habit to develop.

PROVE Safe

PROVE It Safe:

Point the firearm in the safest available direction.

Remove all ammunition.

Observe the chamber.

Verify the feeding path.

Examine the bore for obstructions.

The firearm is now unloaded and safe until it leaves the direct control of the person who unloaded and PROVEd it safe.

Section 1

INTRODUCTION
TO
FIREARMS

1 - INTRODUCTION to FIREARMS

1.1 The Evolution of Firearms

1.1.0 Overview

a. It was probably the Chinese who invented the first explosive powder. They used it in fireworks and rockets. It was also invented at about the same time (the 13th century), by the English alchemist Roger Bacon.

b. People in the Middle Ages quickly learned to use explosive black powder to launch balls or projectiles. They did this by igniting the powder behind a ball or projectile in a cannon (see Figure 1).

c. A cannon is simply a metal tube sealed at one end. Burning powder in the tube produces an expansion of gases. The gas cannot expand against the sealed end. When it expands in the other direction, it pushes the ball ahead of it.

d. A charge of gunpowder was loaded into the bore of early cannons. This was followed by some wadding and a cannonball. Next, some priming powder, or a fuse, was placed in a very small hole or port drilled into the firing chamber.

Figure 1. Cannon

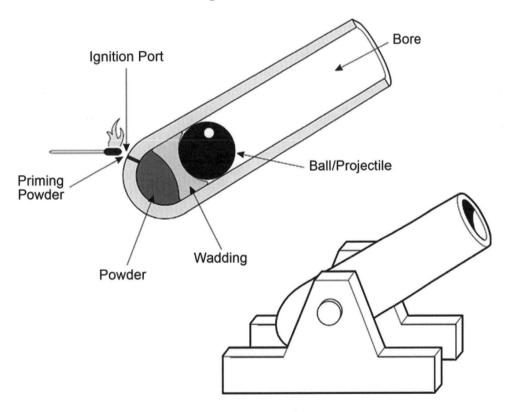

e. A burning match/wick, coal, or spark was touched to the priming powder. The flame travelled down through the port and fired the main powder charge inside the cannon. The explosion launched the cannonball.

f. The use of cannons changed how wars were fought. It also helped change the course of history. Stone castles no longer provided enough protection for the nobility and the villagers living within their walls.

g. During the following centuries, people developed firearms that could be carried and fired by one person. These early firearms had a smooth bore. They could shoot either single or multiple projectiles.

h. The development of these firearms brought about important historical changes. Their use on the battlefield marked the beginning of the end for armoured knights. Because these firearms could be carried, they were also practical for hunting.

1.1.1 Matchlocks

a. One of the earliest carried firearms was the matchlock. It was invented in the early 1400's. The matchlock (see Figure 2) made it possible for the user to aim and fire while holding the firearm with both hands.

b. A slow-burning match/wick activated the matchlock. This match/wick fired the firearm by igniting its priming powder. The match/wick was held by a metal part, called the serpentine, which pivoted at one end.

c. Just below the lit end of the match/wick was the pan. Its job was to hold the priming powder.

d. When the trigger was pulled, the serpentine moved slowly on its pivot. The end holding the burning match/wick dipped it into the priming powder. The priming powder burning through the port fired the main charge of gunpowder in the barrel. The explosion of the main charge launched the projectile.

Figure 2. Matchlock

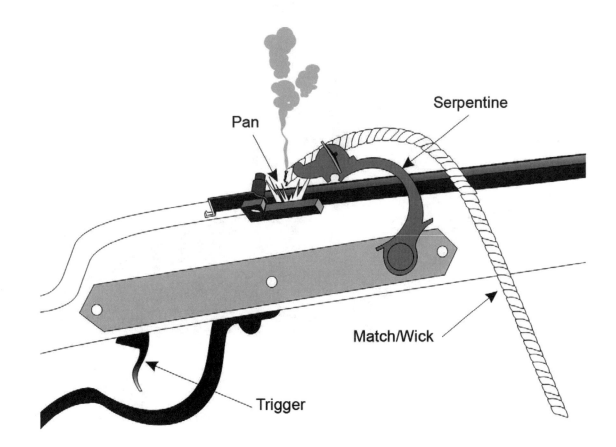

1.1.2 Wheel locks

a. The matchlock had many disadvantages. Rain or high wind could put out the match/wick. Also, having lighted matches/wicks close to gunpowder led to many accidents. Two improved firing systems were developed in the 17th century. These were the wheel lock (see Figure 3) and the flintlock (see Figure 4 in section 1.1.3).

b. The wheel lock firing mechanism worked much like a modern cigarette lighter. A strong spring turned a tooth-edged wheel against a piece of iron pyrite. This caused sparks. The sparks ignited the priming powder. The priming powder fired the main charge.

c. Between shots, the spring was wound up with a key, like a clock. This made the wheel lock ready for instant use, unlike the matchlock. The wheel lock was also safer.

d. However, the mechanism was complex and expensive to make. Also, winding was slow and springs often failed.

Figure 3. Wheel lock

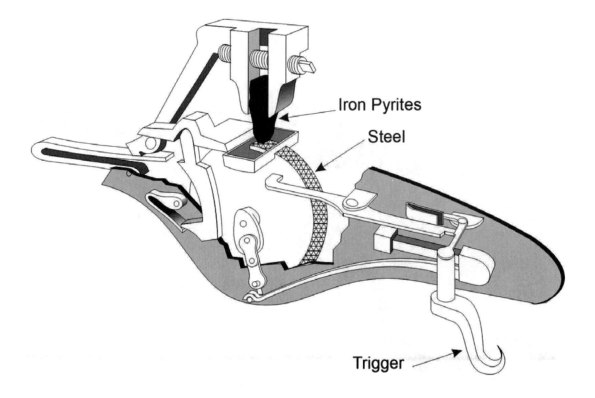

1.1.3 Flintlocks

a. The flintlock has an ignition mechanism similar to the wheel lock. It produced its spark by striking a flint against steel. Since it weighed less and was simpler and cheaper to make, it soon became more popular (see Figure 4).

b. It had a hammer-like part called a cock. Clamped to this cock was the flint. Opposite the flint was the frizzen or steel. When the trigger was pulled, the cock was released. A spring snapped it down to strike the steel with the flint. This produced sparks which fell into the priming powder in the flash pan. These sparks fired the main charge.

Figure 4. Flintlocks

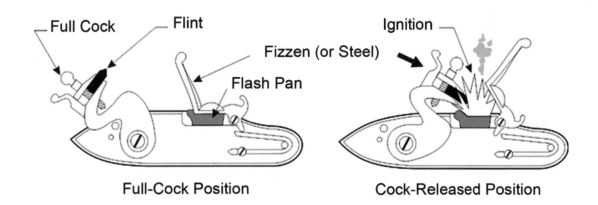

c. For centuries, flintlocks were the standard firearm (see Figures 5a & 5b). During this time, many improvements were introduced. One such improvement of the flintlock over the matchlock and wheel lock was the development of a more reliable ignition system.

d. Other improvements included having more than one barrel, trigger and lock. This enabled the firing of more than one shot before reloading.

Figure 5a. Flintlock pistol

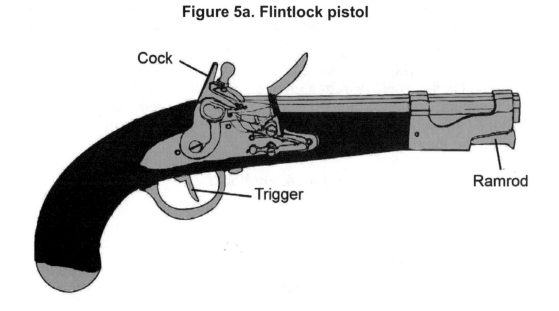

Figure 5b. Flintlock rifle

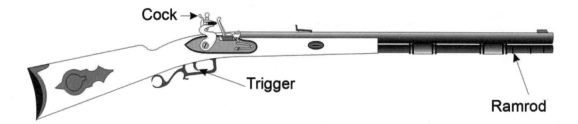

1.1.4 Pistols

a. Between the 15th and 17th centuries, firearms with much shorter barrels were developed. These could be fired with one hand. They were called pistols, probably after the Italian town of Pistoia where many were made.

b. Cavalry soldiers mainly used pistols. They did not need long-range accuracy. Also, pistols were far easier to handle than long guns on the back of a horse. Several could be carried, allowing multiple shots.

c. As new firing mechanisms were developed for long guns, pistols also began using them. Pistols eventually evolved into the various types of modern handguns.

1.1.5 Muskets

a. Muskets were longer-barrelled firearms. They were more accurate at longer ranges than pistols.

b. Muskets usually had smooth bores and could fire either single bullets or a charge of pellets. These pellets were called shot, similar to the projectiles fired by modern shotguns.

1.1.6 Rifles

a. Later, firearms with internally grooved barrels were produced. These were the first rifles.

b. The spiraled-barrel grooving, called rifling, caused the projectile to spin. This improved its stability and accuracy in flight.

c. Rifling was also used in some of the later muzzleloading pistols.

1.1.7 Percussion Caps

a. The percussion cap was developed in the early 1800s (see Figure 6). It was a small metal case (cap) containing material that would explode when struck.

b. When loading the firearm, a percussion cap was placed on a nipple located over the priming port. When struck by the hammer, the cap exploded, igniting the main powder charge through a hole in the nipple.

c. Percussion caps were far more dependable than flintlocks, particularly during stormy weather. They also permitted the development of the first repeating firearms by allowing one trigger and one hammer to discharge multiple barrels.

Figure 6. Percussion cap on a lock

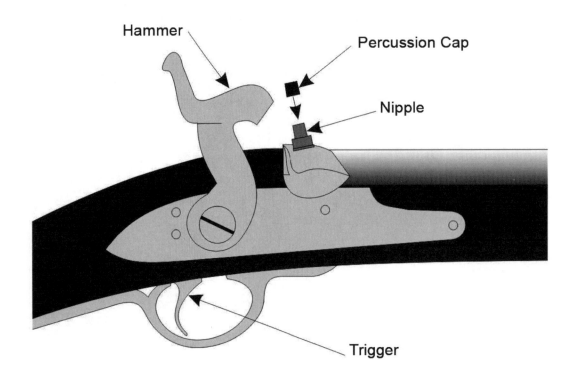

1.1.8 Cartridges

a. All early firearms were muzzleloaders. They loaded through the muzzle. But muzzleloaders were slow to reload. They were also restricted to one shot per barrel.

b. Attempts were made to develop firearms that loaded from the back. They were called breechloaders. However, these early attempts failed because the expanding gases from the burning powder charge leaked back through the breech parts.

c. In the mid 1800s, various cartridge types were developed that made breech loading practical. Eventually, metal cased cartridges similar to modern ones were created (see Figure 7).

d. These cartridges contained the bullet or shot, the main powder charge, and the primer in one package. Pulling the firearm trigger caused the firing pin to strike the primer. The flash from the primer ignited the powder charge. The burning charge caused the cartridge casing to expand. This sealed the breech to prevent gas leakage. The expanding gas launched the projectile down the barrel.

e. Cartridges had at least four advantages:

   - They were easily loaded into the breech.

   - The expanding case prevented gas leakage.

   - They were largely weatherproof.

   - They were more reliable.

f. Cartridges called shells were developed for use in shotguns. These too contain one or more projectiles, powder and primer in one container. In addition, a wad separates the powder from the projectiles. The cartridge casing may be made from metals or other materials such as paper or plastic.

g. Metallic cartridges and shotgun shells were easy to manufacture. Loading firearms also became simpler. This made repeating firearms practical.

Figure 7. Examples of modern cartridges

1.1.9 Repeating Firearms

a. Some types of repeating firearms are listed below:

- Revolvers

- Manually operated rifles and shotguns with magazines containing extra cartridges

- Semi-automatic firearms (the power generated by the fired cartridge causes another cartridge to be chambered after each trigger pull)

- Full-automatic firearms, such as machine guns (firearms which fire continuously as long as the trigger remains pulled and the firearm has a source of ammunition)

See Table 2 in section 1.1.10, which summarizes the main points.

1.1.10 Table 2 - Evolution of Firearms

Table 2. Evolution of Firearms

Evolution of Firearms		
Evolution	**Main Features**	**Limitations**
Matchlock (15th century)	• Used lighted match/wick to fire priming powder • Muzzleloaded	• Match/Wick easily extinguished by rain • Match/Wick burns out • Dangerous around gunpowder • Clumsy • Slow reload • Match/Wick adjustment
Wheel lock (17th century)	• Spring-driven wheel rubbed against iron pyrites to produce sparks • Muzzleloaded • Musket, pistol types and rifles	• Spring required hand winding • Iron pyrites wear out • Mechanism breaks • Heavy, slow reload
Flintlock (17th century)	• Flint snapped against a steel surface to produce spark • Muzzleloaded • Rifling introduced • Paper cartridge introduced	• Flints wear out or break • Springs can fail • Slow reload • Number of shots limited by number of barrels
Percussion cap (19th century)	• Small explosive metal cap replaced flint • More certain of firing • First repeating firearms	• Slow reload • Cap separate from powder and bullet
Metal cartridge (19th century)	• Bullet, powder and primer all in one safe container • Simple, reliable, safe • Breech loading became easy • Smokeless powder introduced	• Requires special equipment to reload cartridge • Easy for unqualified persons to load into a firearm
Breechloading repeaters (19th century)	• Holds and can fire multiple cartridges • Semi-automatics and full automatics introduced	• More danger of an unused cartridge remaining in firearm • More complex mechanisms

1.1.11 Firearms in Canada

a. Since the 16th century, firearms have played a role in the history and development of Canada. They greatly expanded the range and killing power for hunting. People were willing to trade large quantities of furs for firearms and ammunition. "Trade guns" thus became an important factor in the early fur trade. This, in turn, helped open Canada up to the world.

b. Hunting provided a major source of food. It was often critical for survival, especially in poor crop years.

c. Later, the need for hunting to provide food became less necessary for most people for survival. However, many people today still rely on hunting as an important part of their lives.

d. Many have also turned to target shooting. Today, numerous shooting clubs and associations exist. Their members shoot various types of shotguns, rifles or handguns. A wide range of targets from clay to paper also exists.

e. There are also many gun collectors.

1.2 Major Firearm Parts

1.2.0 Overview

a. To use a firearm safely, you must know its parts and understand how they work. The following is a brief introduction to the parts of a firearm. Their functions are explained in more detail in Section 4 - OPERATING FIREARM ACTIONS.

ACTS	Assume every firearm is loaded.

b. Modern firearms consist of three major parts: the barrel, the action, and the stock/frame (see Figure 8).

Figure 8. Major firearms parts

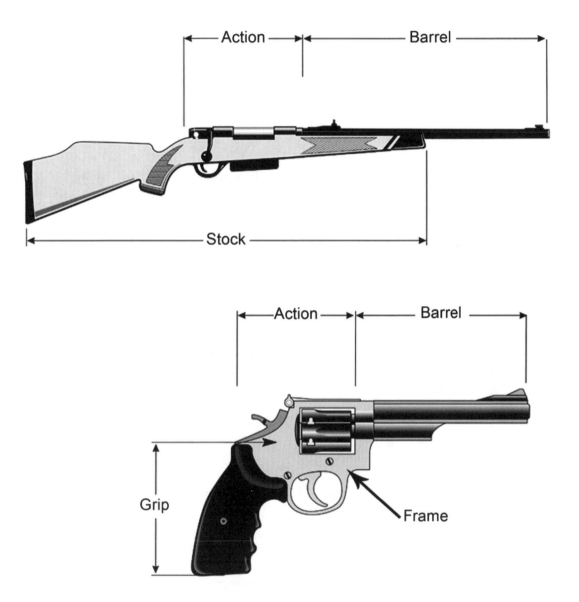

1.2.1 Barrel

a. The *barrel* is a tube, typically made of metal. The bullet or shot travels down this tube when the firearm is fired.

b. Often, manufacturers identify cartridge information required for that firearm on the barrel.

c. The opening at the end of the barrel from which the bullet or shot emerges is called the muzzle.

ACTS	Control the muzzle direction at all times.

1.2.2 Action

a. The action contains the parts that do the following:

- Chamber the cartridge.

- Fire the ammunition.

- Extract the unfired cartridges and used casings.

1.2.3 Trigger

a. *Triggers, safeties* and *magazines* are all parts of the action.

b. The *trigger* releases the part of the action that fires the cartridge. The *trigger guard* is a rigid loop around the trigger made to protect it and prevent anything from accidentally touching the trigger.

ACTS	**Trigger finger must be kept off the trigger and out of the trigger guard.**

1.2.4 Safeties

a. Safeties usually block some part of the action to prevent firing. Some firearms do not have safeties.

b. The safety should be **ON** whenever a firearm is loaded. It should only be moved to **OFF** when required.

c. Some safeties may also act as decocking levers.

 Never rely on the safety to prevent firing. A loaded firearm with the safety ON could still fire. All mechanical devices can fail; safeties can wear down and may not operate properly.

1.2.5 Magazine

a. The magazine is a device that holds cartridges in repeating firearms. The location of the magazine depends on the make and model of the firearm.

b. The magazine can be either fixed or removable.

1.2.6 Stock or Grip

a. The *stock* or *grip* is the handle of the firearm. Most are made of wood or a synthetic material.

b. Stocks and grips are designed to automatically align your finger with the trigger when you pick up the firearm. This is why it is so easy to accidentally put your finger into the trigger guard without thinking.

ACT**S**	**S**ee that the firearm is unloaded - PROVE it safe.

1.3 The Firing Sequence

a. Just about all modern firearms follow the same firing sequence (see Figure 9):

1. A squeeze on the trigger releases the firing mechanism. This results in the firing pin striking the primer of the cartridge.

2. When struck by the firing pin, the primer explodes. This projects a flame into the cartridge body.

3. The flame from the primer ignites the powder. The powder burns and produces rapidly expanding gases.

4. The high-pressure gas drives the bullet or shot forward down the barrel.

Figure 9. Firing sequence

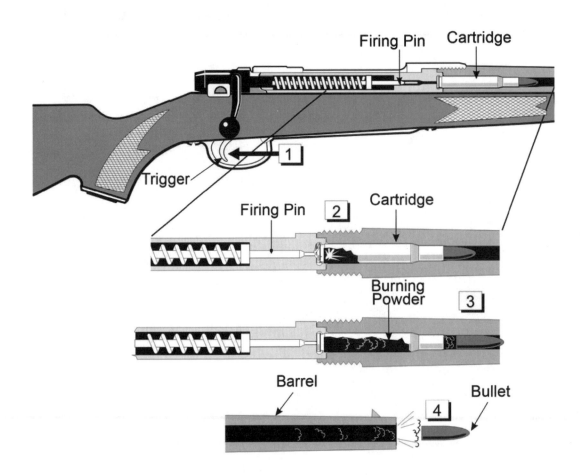

1.4 Types of Firearm Actions

a. Firearms vary in design, depending on their purpose. Some are made for target shooting. Others are used for hunting birds or small game. Still others are for hunting big game.

b. The three common types of firearms are as follows:

- Shotguns
- Rifles
- Handguns

c. The basic types of actions (see Figure 10) used in these firearms are as follows:

- Hinge (or break) action
- Bolt action
- Lever action
- Pump action
- Semi-automatic action
- Revolving action

d. Some firearms have several barrels. Typically, these are shotguns or combination shotguns/rifles.

Figure 10. Types of firearms actions

Hinge (or Break) Action Shotgun

Bolt Action Rifle

Lever Action Rifle

Pump Action Shotgun

Semi-Automatic Rifle

Double Action
Revolver

Single Action
Semi-Automatic

1.5 Legal Responsibilities

a. Various laws, regulations and restrictions govern your activities as an owner or user of a firearm. They set minimum standards of conduct, and you have a responsibility to know, understand and obey them.

1.6 Classes of Firearms

a. The classes of firearms are as follows:

- Non-restricted

- Restricted

- Prohibited

b. Legal requirements for a particular firearm depend on the class to which it belongs. Prohibited firearms are subject to the most stringent controls, restricted firearms are controlled to a lesser extent and non-restricted firearms are the least regulated of the three classes.

c. Although most airguns are not included in the provisions of the *Firearms Act*, they must be treated as firearms in respect of safe practices, such as the **Vital Four ACTS.**

⚠ **The Vital Four ACTS of firearm safety apply to all classes of firearms.**

1.7 Review Questions

1. What are two differences between muzzleloaders and modern firearm designs?

2. What purpose is served by the grooves cut in the bore of a barrel?

3. What are the six types of actions?

4. What are the three classes of firearms?

NOTES:

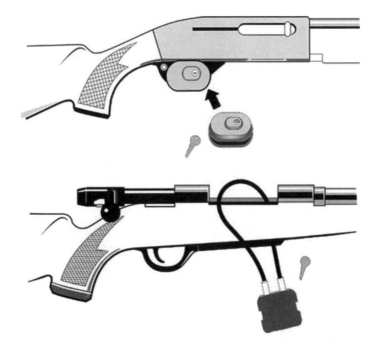

Section 2

BASIC SAFETY

2 - BASIC SAFETY

2.1 The Vital Four ACTS

2.1.0 Overview

a. Almost all firearm accidents can be prevented by following some basic safety rules.

b. The most important of these are the **Vital Four ACTS** (see Table 3). You may want to think of these rules as acts you must carry out.

Table 3. The Vital Four ACTS of Firearm Safety

The Vital Four ACTS of Firearm Safety	
	Assume every firearm is loaded. • Regard any firearm as a potential danger.
	Control the muzzle direction at all times. • Identify the safest available muzzle direction. • Keep the firearm pointed in the safest available direction. • The muzzle of a firearm should not be pointed towards yourself or any other person.
	Trigger finger must be kept off the trigger and out of the trigger guard. • Resist the temptation to put your finger on the trigger or inside the trigger guard when you pick up a firearm. • Accidental discharge is far more likely to occur if your finger is on the trigger or inside the trigger guard.
	See that the firearm is unloaded - **PROVE** it safe. • Do not handle the firearm unless you can properly **PROVE** it safe. • Check to see that both chamber and magazine are empty. Do this every time you handle a firearm, for any reason. • Pass or accept only open and unloaded firearms. This is an important habit to develop.

2.1.1 PROVE Safe

PROVE it safe:

- **P**oint the firearm in the safest available direction

- **R**emove all ammunition

- **O**bserve the chamber

- **V**erify the feeding path

- **E**xamine the bore for obstructions.

The firearm is now unloaded and safe until it leaves the direct control of the person who unloaded and PROVEd it safe.

2.2 Basic Firearm Safety Practices

2.2.0 Overview

a. While many safety practices have been incorporated into the **Firearms Act** and **Regulations,** experienced firearm users often exceed those requirements by following some or all of the recommended safety practices listed in the sections below. These safety practices are summarized in Table 11 in Section 8.6. (For specific requirements on storage and transport, see Section 9 - SAFE STORAGE DISPLAY, TRANSPORTATION & HANDLING OF NON-RESTRICTED FIREARMS).

2.2.1 Keep Firearms and Ammunition Separate and Secure When Not In Use

a. Some of the recommended safety practices are listed below:

- Firearms under your care and control are your responsibility 24 hours a day.

- Firearms are safer when stored and transported under lock and key. Examples include trigger or cable locks, and securely locked containers.

- In many cases, you are required by law to have your firearm unloaded and properly locked. Be aware of what the law says about which firearms need to be locked and when.

- Keep firearms and ammunition out of sight during transport and storage. This will reduce the chances of theft. It will also prevent unqualified or unauthorized persons from using them. Ammunition and firearms must be kept away from unsupervised children. Accidental misuse can cause a tragedy.

- Store firearms unloaded. Store ammunition separately. Lock the firearm and the ammunition separately when storing them.

2.2.2 Load a Firearm Only for Actual Use

a. Some of the recommended safety practices are listed below:

- A firearm should be loaded only when you intend to use it and where it can be safely and legally discharged. At all other times, it should be unloaded.

- Load a firearm only when you have reached the shooting area and you are ready to shoot. Completely unload the firearm before you leave the shooting area.

- Always make sure a firearm is unloaded before you pass it to anyone or anytime it leaves your hands. Whenever possible, leave the action open.

- Never accept a loaded firearm from anyone.

- Never run with a loaded firearm. Never climb or cross an obstacle with a loaded firearm. Never jump a ditch with a loaded firearm.

- Never toss or drop a firearm across a ditch or fence.

- Do not lean loaded firearms against a vehicle, tree or wall. They could fall and accidentally discharge.

- Transport only unloaded firearms by vehicle or boat. Many accidents occur as firearms are being stored or removed from a vehicle. Also, the motion of the vehicle or boat can make you stumble or drop the firearm. Either way, it can fire accidentally if it is loaded.

- Always unload a firearm before transport or storage. This prevents accidental discharge if the firearm is bumped during transport. It also reduces the chances of unexpected firing by an unqualified user.

2.2.3 Be Sure Before You Shoot

a. Some of the recommended safety practices are listed below:

- Always use your firearm in the safest manner possible. Be sure of your target and beyond before you shoot.

- Always examine the bore for obstructions before loading.

- Always check that you are using the right ammunition. Use only the ammunition for which the firearm was designed. Carry only the type of ammunition you intend to shoot.

- Never rely on the firearm's safety. Safeties wear down and may not work properly. Also, a loaded firearm may fire even with the safety on. All mechanical devices can fail.

2.2.4 Be Sure of Your Target and Beyond

a. To be sure of your target and beyond, follow the recommendations below:

- Positively identify your target. Make sure it is exactly what you want to shoot.

- Do not shoot when in doubt. Never fire at a movement, a colour, a sound or a shape.

- Check that you have a clear field of fire.

- Check that the area behind your target is safe before shooting.

- Never use a scope as a substitute for binoculars to identify persons, animals or objects.

b. Always be aware of where your bullet or shot may end up. This is your responsibility. A bullet or shot may ricochet. It may also travel far beyond the target. If you are unsure, check the following recommendations:

- Never shoot if your bullet may hit a hard surface or water. Both can cause a bullet or fragments to ricochet in unsafe directions.

- Never shoot at a target near a building.

- Never shoot at a target on top of a hill.

- Only shoot when you are sure no one is ahead of you.

2.3 Secure Locking Devices

a. Secure locking devices prevent a firearm from being fired (see Figure 11). To work effectively, they must be installed properly. Please note that not all secure locking devices are compatible with each firearm.

b. In some cases, they are required by law (see Section 9 – SAFE STORAGE, DISPLAY, TRANSPORTATION & HANDLING OF NON-RESTRICTED FIREARMS). Several devices are available for this purpose. The most common are key and combination trigger locks, and chain or cable locks. All of these locks block operation. Check with a firearms dealer for a locking device best suited for your specific firearm.

Figure 11. Various firearm locking devices

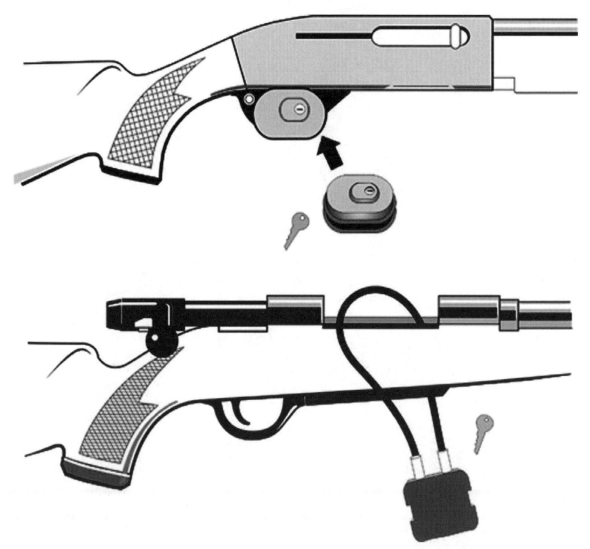

2.4 Review Questions

1. State the **Vital Four ACTS** of firearm safety.

2. When you have ammunition in the home, how should it be stored?

3. Why is it necessary to store a firearm and its ammunition separately?

4. Are you familiar with a firearms-related accident? If so, how could it have been prevented?

NOTES:

Section 3

AMMUNITION

3 - AMMUNITION

3.0 Overview

a. This section discusses black powder, rifle cartridges, and shotgun shells. This will help you choose the right ammunition. You should only carry ammunition that suits the firearm you are using and the target you intend to shoot. This applies whether you are hunting or target shooting.

b. For more detailed information, consult a firearms dealer or a gunsmith.

3.1 Rifling

a. Rifled barrels have a series of spiral grooves inside the barrel. The ridges of metal between the grooves are called lands. The lands and grooves together make up the rifling (see Figure 12).

b. Rifling makes the bullet spin as it leaves the barrel so it will be stable in flight.

3.2 Calibre

a. Rifled firearms are sized by calibre. Calibre is a measurement of bore diameter in either hundredths of an inch (Imperial) or millimetres (Metric). The distance could be measured either in inches or millimetres from land-to-land or from groove-to-groove, depending on the specific cartridge (see Figure 12).

 Always consult the data stamp on the barrel of your firearm to find out the exact name of the ammunition that fits it.

Figure 12. Rifled versus smooth-bore barrels

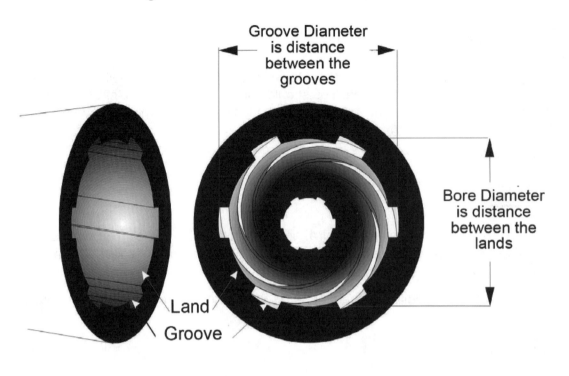

Rifled Barrel

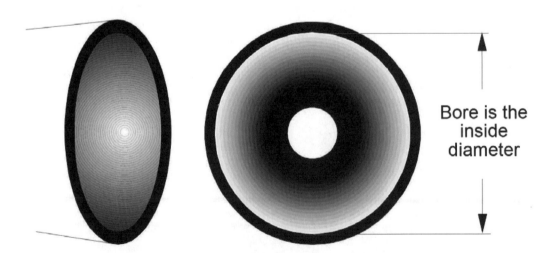

Smooth-Bore Barrel

3.3 Choke

a. Except in the case of a rifled barrel, the bore of a shotgun barrel is usually smooth and may be narrowed at the muzzle end. This narrowing is called the choke.

b. The choke of a shotgun barrel helps control the spread of the shot after it is fired. This is very much like the way the nozzle of a hose controls the spray of water.

c. The pattern of the pellets on the target is affected by the choke.

   - Full choke produces a tight pattern.

   - Modified choke produces a more open pattern.

   - Improved cylinder produces an even more open pattern.

   - Cylinder bore produces the most open pattern.

d. A shotgun barrel which has no choke or narrowing at the end of the barrel is called a cylinder bore. It is often used for larger pellet sizes such as buckshot or slugs.

See Figure 13 for the uses of the various chokes and their shot patterns. The pattern will depend on the different type of shot used, for example: lead, steel, bismuth or tungsten-iron. It is the shooter's responsibility to learn about the shotgun pattern.

Figure 13. Cross-section view of various chokes and illustration of shotgun patterns (30" patterning target)

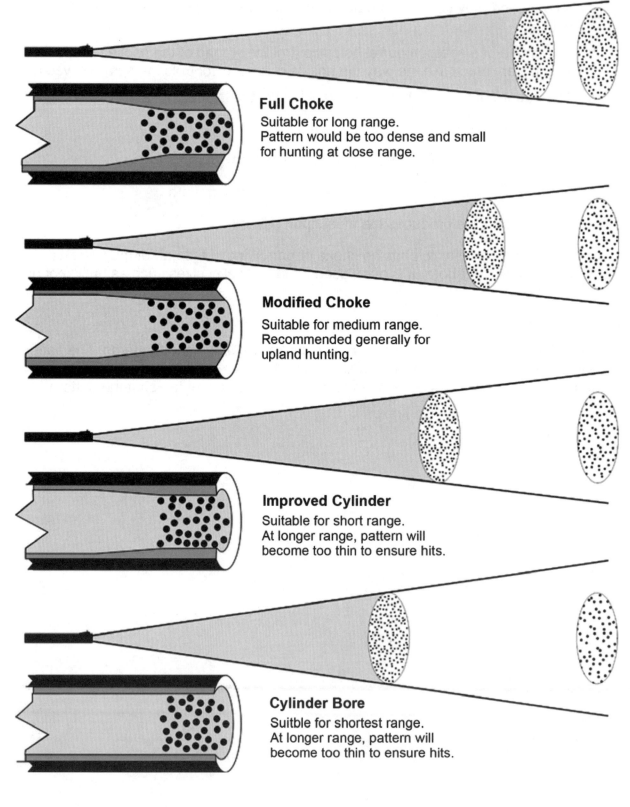

Full Choke

Suitable for long range.
Pattern would be too dense and small
for hunting at close range.

Modified Choke

Suitable for medium range.
Recommended generally for
upland hunting.

Improved Cylinder

Suitable for short range.
At longer range, pattern will
become too thin to ensure hits.

Cylinder Bore

Suitble for shortest range.
At longer range, pattern will
become too thin to ensure hits.

3.4 Shotgun Barrels

a. The use of smooth slugs, rifled slugs, and slugs contained in a sabot or plastic sleeve, is becoming more common in modern shotguns. This allows shotguns to fire single projectiles similar to a rifle.

b. Previously, some shotguns were manufactured with adjustable chokes. Some modern shotguns are made with interchangeable choke tubes. On these models, the choke can be changed simply by unscrewing a removable tube at the muzzle of the barrel and replacing it with another tube with a different choke.

c. One shotgun with interchangeable chokes or barrels can be used for skeet or clay target shooting, migratory waterfowl, upland game birds, protection from dangerous animals and large game hunting, depending on the ammunition used and the regulations in the area.

d. The rifled choke is becoming popular. This is an interchangeable choke tube that is fitted to the muzzle where the choke tubes are screwed in. The rifled choke provides the option of using a smooth slug, a rifled slug or a sabot slug. The rifled choke tube is designed to make the projectiles spin as they leave the muzzle. This makes them more like a normal rifle bullet, increasing accuracy and useful distance.

e. Rifled shotgun barrels are identical to a normal rifle barrel except they have the bore diameter of the gauge of the shotgun. This has resulted in better accuracy and new uses for shotguns.

Figure 14. Types of shotgun slugs

 Slug

Rifled Slug

Sabot Slug

Rounded Slug

3.5 Shotgun Gauge

a. Shotgun barrels are sized by gauge instead of calibre. Gauge is an older system of measurement and is calculated by the number of lead balls (each having the same diameter as the bore) that weigh one pound. In other words, if it took 12 balls with the same diameter as a bore to make one pound, a shotgun with that bore would be called a 12-gauge shotgun. One exception to this rule is the .410-cal. shotgun. It is measured as a calibre because it was developed later (see Figure 15). Note that .410 calibre is now frequently marked on modern ammunition boxes as .410 gauge.

Figure 15. Shotgun gauge (not to scale)

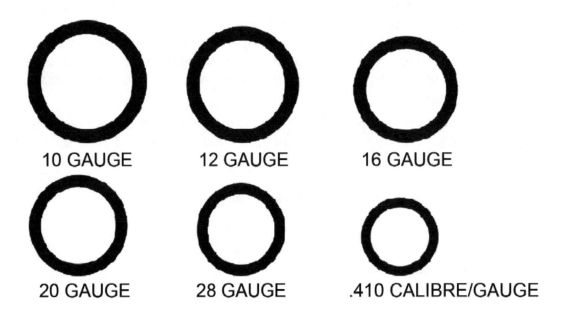

10 GAUGE   12 GAUGE   16 GAUGE

20 GAUGE   28 GAUGE   .410 CALIBRE/GAUGE

3.6 Black Powder and Projectiles

3.6.1 Black Powder

a. Muzzleloading firearms use black powder and lead balls as ammunition. There are also black powder substitutes.

b. Black powder is available in four different types (see Table 4).

Table 4. Types of Black Powder

Types of Black Powder	
Fg	Very coarse granules of powder. Used in larger bore muskets.
FFg	Finer granules than the Fg. Used in muzzleloading shotguns, big-bore rifles and single-shot pistols of .45 calibre and up.
FFFg	Finer granules than the FFg and the most common type. Used in nearly all cap and ball revolvers.
FFFFg	The finest granules. Used only in the priming pans of flintlocks.

c. Remember, the finer the granules of powder, the more pressure it creates when fired.

 Never use FFFFg powder as anything other than a priming powder.

d. Black powder ignites very easily. A glowing coal, a spark, even static electricity or a sharp blow may ignite it. Handle black powder with great care, especially when transporting it. Black powder should be stored in a secure, cool, dry place, and always in its original container.

e. As black powder ages, it becomes more unstable. When stored for long periods, the granules will begin to cake together and white crystals will form. When this happens, the black powder has become very unstable. It should be soaked immediately in water.

 Black powder ignites easily. Always handle with extreme care and wear eye protection. Never have a source of ignition around powder. Never smoke near black powder. Glowing embers may be present in the bore after firing a black powder firearm. An explosion hazard could be created if you proceed immediately to reload. Never interchange smokeless powder and black powder. Use them only in firearms intended for their use.

3.6.2 Black Powder Projectiles for a Muzzleloading Firearm

a. Modern black powder or muzzleloading firearms shoot four different types (see Figure 16) of projectiles as follows:

- Spherical - a round ball, usually loaded along with a lubricated patch, which seals the barrel around the ball

- Conical - cylindrical-shaped projectiles known as Mini-balls, they have a hollow base that expands to seal the gases when the firearm fires

- Shot - pellets of assorted sizes and materials

- Sabot - plastic or synthetic carrier that encases a projectile.

Figure 16. Ammunition components for a muzzleloader

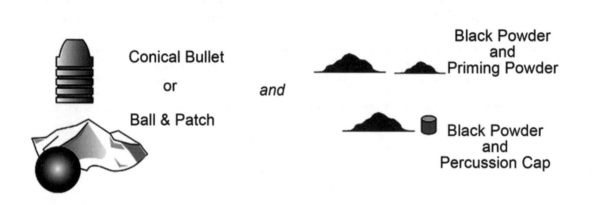

3.7 Cartridges ✳

3.7.0 Overview

a. A cartridge is the ammunition used in a rifle or a handgun. Two kinds of cartridges commonly available are: rim-fire and centre-fire. These terms describe where the primer is located at the base of the cartridge casing. They also describe where the firing pin strikes (see Figure 17).

Figure 17. Example of a rim-fire and centre-fire cartridge with head stamp

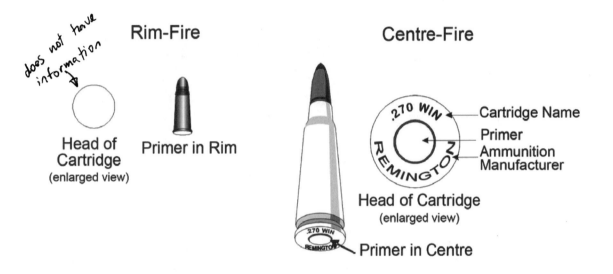

b. Manufacturers produce firearms of many calibres. Always make sure the cartridge name matches the information in the data stamp, if available, on the barrel of the firearm (see Figure 18). This is the most important point to remember. Then, choose the right type of ammunition for your firearm and target. The right shape or weight of the bullet is an example. If in doubt, consult a firearms or ammunition dealer.

c. If there is no data stamp, take the firearm to a qualified individual. They can measure the chamber and advise on proper ammunition. Additional information is available from manufacturers' catalogues and brochures.

Figure 18. Example of a barrel data stamp

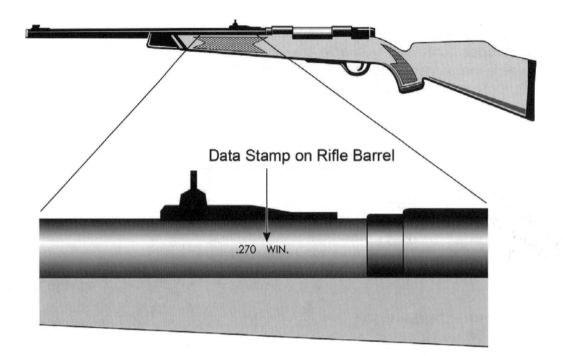

Data Stamp on Rifle Barrel

.270 WIN.

Some firearms may not have a data stamp. Or, they may have an incorrect stamp. Some firearms may have been altered and the existing data stamp may be incorrect. They should be checked by a qualified individual before use. If you are re-loading your own ammunition, you must strictly follow the instructions and procedures outlined in the manuals provided for this process. Visually inspect all ammunition for defects before loading.

d. Many firearm owners load their own centre-fire ammunition. This allows them to save money and create a high quality product made specifically for their firearm and shooting conditions. If you are handloading your own ammunition, you must strictly follow the instructions and procedures outlined in the manuals provided for this process.

e. Incorrectly loaded ammunition may cause the firearm to malfunction or jam. Malfunctions could lead to an accident. The firearm could blow up and injure the shooter. Do not accept or use reloaded cartridges unless you know that they were made and reloaded correctly.

3.7.1 Cartridge Components and Materials

a. Ammunition varies in size, appearance and materials. Ammunition cartridges for rifles are made up of four basic components described below. See Figures 19 & 20 below, Figure 21 in section 3.7.2 and Chart 1 in section 3.7.5).

Table 5. Cartridge Components and Materials

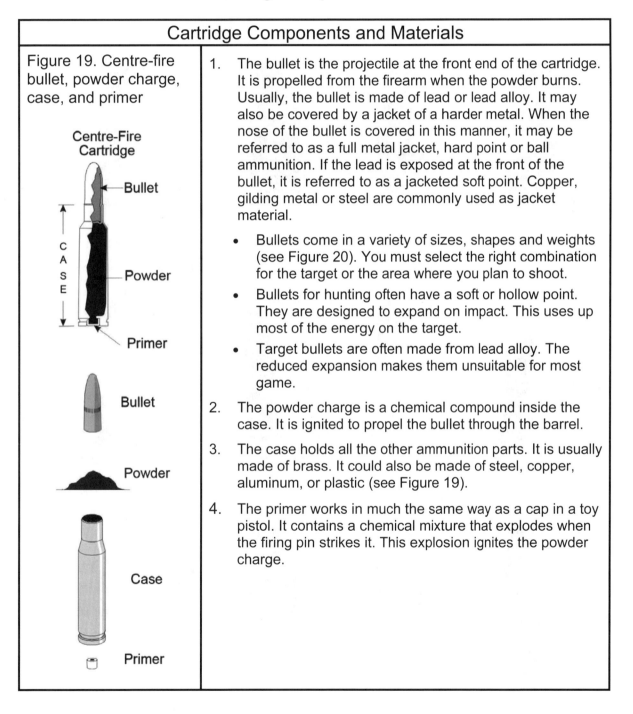

Cartridge Components and Materials	
Figure 19. Centre-fire bullet, powder charge, case, and primer	1. The bullet is the projectile at the front end of the cartridge. It is propelled from the firearm when the powder burns. Usually, the bullet is made of lead or lead alloy. It may also be covered by a jacket of a harder metal. When the nose of the bullet is covered in this manner, it may be referred to as a full metal jacket, hard point or ball ammunition. If the lead is exposed at the front of the bullet, it is referred to as a jacketed soft point. Copper, gilding metal or steel are commonly used as jacket material. • Bullets come in a variety of sizes, shapes and weights (see Figure 20). You must select the right combination for the target or the area where you plan to shoot. • Bullets for hunting often have a soft or hollow point. They are designed to expand on impact. This uses up most of the energy on the target. • Target bullets are often made from lead alloy. The reduced expansion makes them unsuitable for most game. 2. The powder charge is a chemical compound inside the case. It is ignited to propel the bullet through the barrel. 3. The case holds all the other ammunition parts. It is usually made of brass. It could also be made of steel, copper, aluminum, or plastic (see Figure 19). 4. The primer works in much the same way as a cap in a toy pistol. It contains a chemical mixture that explodes when the firing pin strikes it. This explosion ignites the powder charge.

＊303 British and
303 Savage are not
interchangeable

＊　**Figure 20. Examples of rifle bullets**

RIFLE BULLETS

■ LEAD　　■ COPPER

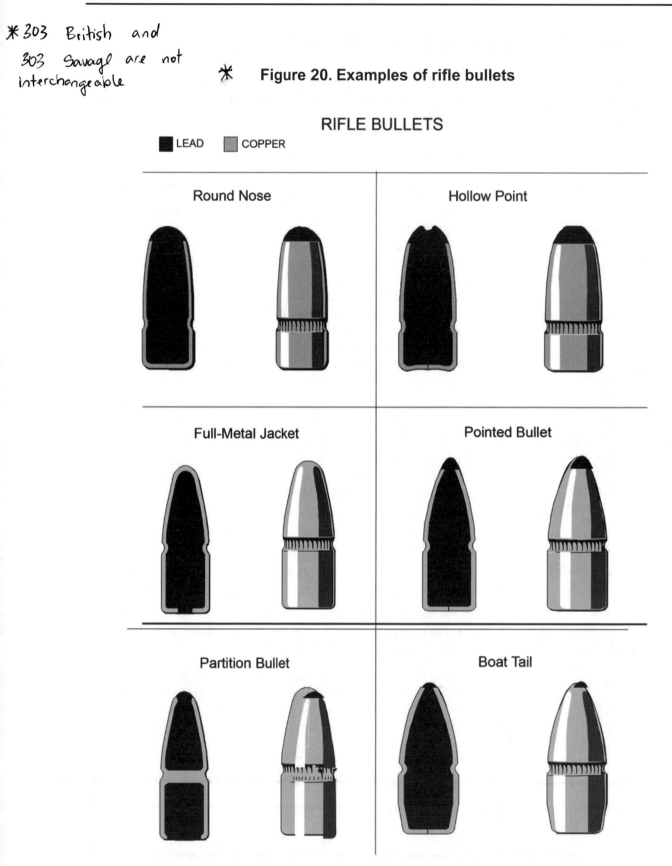

Round Nose

Hollow Point

Full-Metal Jacket

Pointed Bullet

Partition Bullet

Boat Tail

3.7.2 Types of Cartridges

a. There are two basic types of modern cartridges: rim-fire and centre-fire.

   1. **Rim-fire** ammunition's priming chemical fills the space inside the bottom rim of a thin brass or copper cartridge casing. The soft rim dents when struck by the firing pin. This crushes the priming compound. It explodes, and this ignites the powder (see Figure 21).

      • All popular modern rim-fire cartridges are .22 calibre. They commonly come in BB, short, long, and long rifle. A .22-magnum cartridge is also available, however, it is not interchangeable with the other .22 cartridges. Be sure to use the correct ammunition for your specific firearm.

      • Rim-fire cartridge bullets generally are made of lead. They are lubricated with grease or special waxes that reduce the build-up of lead in the rifle barrel.

 Dry firing any firearm can damage the firearm. Dry firing means to initiate live firing without a cartridge in the chamber.

Figure 21. Rim-fire cartridge

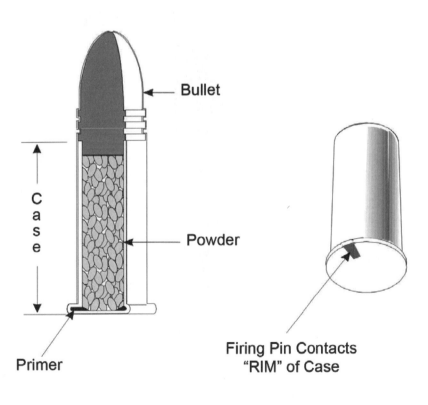

2. **Centre-fire** ammunition (see Figure 22) is used for higher power firearms. The primer is located in a separate cup at the base of the case. The firing pin strikes the primer. This explodes the priming compound. This in turn ignites the powder charge.

Figure 22. Centre-fire cartridge

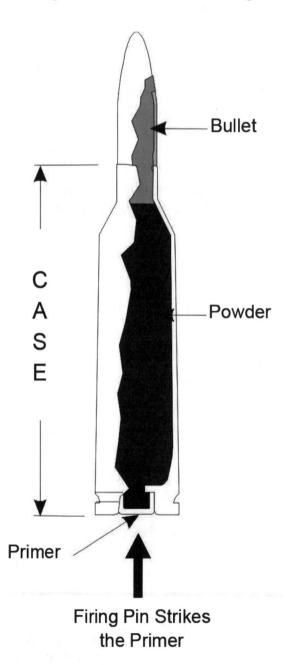

Bullet

C
A
S
E

Powder

Primer

Firing Pin Strikes
the Primer

3.7.3 Cartridge Names

a. There are various ways of identifying or "naming" cartridges. Some cartridges have several names. The cartridge name, or an abbreviation of it, is stamped on the head of the case. It is also found printed on the ammunition manufacturer's box (see Figure 23).

b. Historically, cartridge names contained their approximate calibres. Calibre refers to the diameter of the bore. Calibre may be measured in fractions of an inch or in metric. Historically, inch dimensions (example .308 calibre) were measured from the top of one land to the top of the opposite land, known as land-to-land. Metric dimensions (example 7 mm) were measured from the bottom of one groove to the bottom of the opposite groove, known as groove-to-groove.

c. Currently, modern firearms include the length of the cartridge casing in the description of the cartridge to identify the name of the ammunition that the firearm is designed to use. This is done to tell the difference between cartridges having the same calibre but different cartridge casings. **For example, cartridges with different names are not interchangeable (.303 Savage and .303 British, 7-mm Mauser and 7-mm Remington Magnum, .300 Savage and .300 Win Mag).** ✳

d. Because a manufacturer may choose to make a firearm or ammunition in a cartridge originally made by another manufacturer, confusion can occur. For example, you can use a Remington rifle to fire a .300 Winchester Magnum cartridge made by the Federal Cartridge Company (see Figure 23).

e. The head stamp includes very valuable information, such as the cartridge name. It may also tell you the following:

- The calibre

- The manufacturer

- Whether the ammunition is regular or magnum and any other relevant details

f. Always read the cartridge name head stamp. It is the only way to be sure that the cartridge matches the firearm. If in doubt, check with a gunsmith or gun shop.

g. The term magnum comes from the description of a large bottle of wine. It was first applied to large bottleneck cartridges that produced greater power than was the normal standard for that calibre. Today, it is more a marketing term than a technical term, but is an important part of the name.

⚠ **Some ammunition may not have a cartridge name head stamp such as rim-fire cartridges. Also, some privately reloaded ammunition may no longer match the original stamp. Whenever possible, refer to the information on the ammunition box. If in doubt, have any such ammunition checked by a qualified individual before you use it.**

Figure 23. Cartridge head stamp, data stamp and ammunition box label

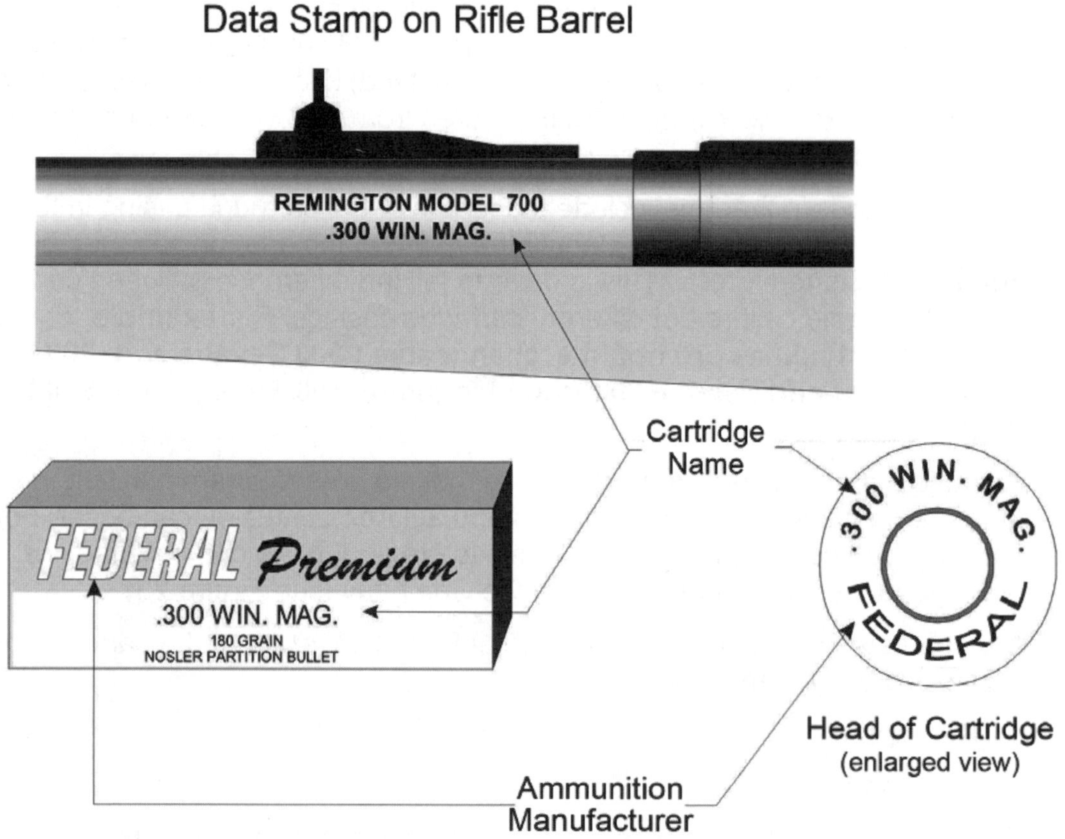

Data Stamp on Rifle Barrel

REMINGTON MODEL 700
.300 WIN. MAG.

Cartridge
Name

FEDERAL Premium
.300 WIN. MAG.
180 GRAIN
NOSLER PARTITION BULLET

.300 WIN. MAG.
FEDERAL

Head of Cartridge
(enlarged view)

Ammunition
Manufacturer

3.7.4 Table 6 - Typical Cartridge Names and Actual Diameters

a. Table 6 shows some examples of ammunition. As can be seen in the table, cartridge names are often similar. Many different names may fit the same calibre. It is absolutely essential to read the whole name of a cartridge before you select it.

Table 6. Typical Cartridge Names and Actual Diameters

Name	Calibre	Bullet Diameter	Original Manufacturer or Major User
7-mm Rem. Mag.	7-mm cal.	.284"	Remington
.30-30 Win.	.30 cal.	.308"	Winchester
.308 Win.	.30 cal.	.308"	Winchester
.30-06	.30 cal.	.308"	U.S. Government
.303 Sav.	.30 cal.	.308"	Savage
.303 Brit.	.303 cal.	.311"	British Army
.44 Rem. Mag	.44 cal.	.429"	Remington
.45-70 Gov.	.45 cal.	.458"	U.S. Government

 Never use incorrect ammunition in your firearm, for example:

- **Never use .303 Savage cartridges in firearms chambered for .303 British. The smaller Savage cartridge may burst the case.**
- **Serious injury to the shooter and significant damage to the firearm may occur.**
- **This dangerous situation can happen with other calibres, as well.**

b. To choose the right cartridge for the type of target and firearm, follow the manufacturer's recommendations. For rifle ammunition, these recommendations can be found in catalogues. The catalogues are distributed through sporting goods stores and gun shops.

3.7.5 Chart 1 - Comparison of Rifle Cartridges and Shotgun Shells

Chart 1. Comparison of rifle cartridges and shotgun shells

TYPE	COMPONENTS	PURPOSE	USES
CARTRIDGE		**USED IN RIFLES**	
Rim-Fire or Centre-Fire Sizes: Calibre e.g. - .22 or .30 or 7 mm	CASE	Contains components	Target Shooting
	PRIMER	Fires powder charge when struck by firing pin	Hunting
			Military
	POWDER	Burns and expands to propel bullet	Police
	BULLET	Strikes target	Collecting
SHELL		**USED IN SHOTGUNS**	
Sizes: Gauge e.g. - 12 or 20 gauge or .410 cal. 2¾", 3, 3½" approximate case length *after* firing.	HULL	Contains components	
	PRIMER	Fires powder charge when struck by firing pin	Hunting
			Target Shooting
	POWDER	Burns and expands to propel shot or slug	Collecting
	WAD	Separates shot from powder and seals barrel behind shot during firing	Military
	SHOT or SLUG	Spreads out to strike target / Strikes target	Police

3.8 Shotgun Shells

3.8.0 Overview

a. A shotgun cartridge is commonly called a "shell ". It is usually measured by gauge, not calibre.

b. Shotgun ammunition is centre-fire. The casing or hull has a thick, solid base. The primer is located in a separate cup in the centre bottom of the casing.

c. The firing pin strikes the primer. This explodes the priming compound and ignites the powder. The shot charge is usually a number of pellets. It can also be a single slug.

3.8.1 Shotgun Shell Components and Materials

a. Shotgun shell components are similar to those of rifle and handgun cartridges. However, there are five components, not four (see Figures 24 & 25 below and Chart 1 in section 3.7.5). The five shotgun components are described below:

1. Shot is the name for the charge of pellets fired from a shotgun. Shot may be either lead, steel, bismuth or tungsten-iron pellets. Historically, shot was primarily made of lead. However, because of environmental concerns, use of other materials is increasing:

   • The use of steel in some shotgun barrels may cause damage to the firearm. For further information, please check the manufacturer's manual or contact a gunsmith.

   • The size and number of pellets vary. They depend on the type and range of the target. Smaller pellets are usually used for smaller or closer targets (see Figure 26 in section 3.8.3).

   • Sometimes a single large projectile known as a "**slug**" is fired from a shotgun. This is for hunting larger game.

2. Shotgun shells also contain one or more **wads**. The wad is made of paper, fibre or plastic. It separates the powder charge from the shot or slug. This prevents hot gas from damaging the shot and seals the gases behind the charge. It also separates the shot from the inside of the barrel.

3. The **powder charge** is a chemical compound in the body of the hull. It is ignited to propel the shot through the barrel.

4. The **hull** contains all the other ammunition components. The hull is commonly made of a combination of brass, plastic or paper.

5. The **primer** contains a chemical mixture that explodes when the firing pin strikes it. This ignites the powder charge.

Figure 24. Shotgun shell components

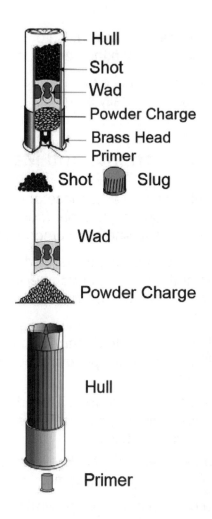

Figure 25. Shotgun shells

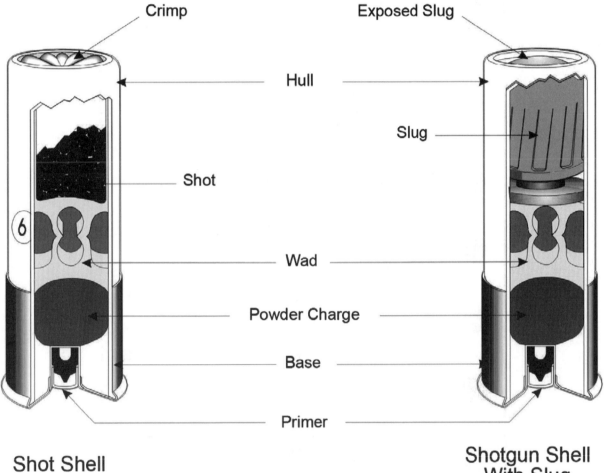

Crimp

Exposed Slug

Hull

Slug

Shot

Wad

Powder Charge

Base

Primer

Shot Shell

Shotgun Shell
With Slug

3.8.2 Chart 2 - Shot Sizes

Chart 2. Shot sizes

Shot Sizes

Buckshot Sizes				Shot Sizes			
	Shot Number	Diameter in Inches	# Pellets Typical Loads		Shot Number	Diameter in Inches	Pellets / oz. Lead	Pellets / oz. Steel

Buckshot Sizes

Shot Number	Diameter in Inches	# Pellets Typical Loads
4	.24	27 34
3	.25	20 24
1	.30	12 16 20 24
0	.32	12
00	.33	9 12 15
000	.36	8

Shot Sizes

Shot Number	Diameter in Inches	Pellets / oz. Lead	Pellets / oz. Steel
9	.08	585	na
8	.09	410	na
7½	.095	350	na
7	.10	-	420
6	.11	225	316
5	.12	170	243
4	.13	135	191
3	.14	-	153
2	.15	87	125
1	.16	-	103
B	.17	-	na
BB	.18	50	72
BBB	.19	-	61
T	.20	-	53
TT	.21	-	na
F	.22	-	na

3.8.3 Shotgun Shell Types

a. Various types of shells exist. They vary in length and gauge, and in size and type of pellet (shot). See Chart 2 in section 3.8.2. To choose the right ammunition for your firearm and target, follow the manufacturer's recommendations.

For example, shotgun shells in 12 gauge commonly come in several lengths as follows:

- 2¾ in. (70 mm)
- 3 in. (76 mm)
- 3½ in. (89 mm)

Note: These dimensions refer to the lengths of the shells after firing (see Figure 26).

Figure 26. Shotgun shells and fired hulls

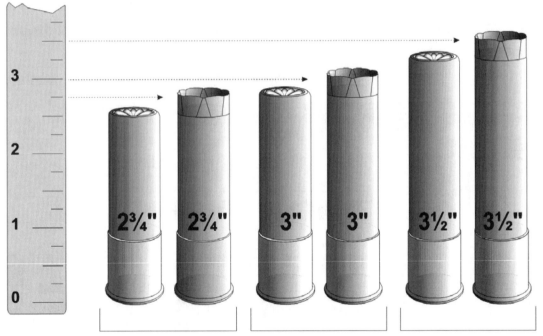

12-Gauge Shotgun Shells Unfired and Fired

⚠ **It should be noted that some European shotguns are manufactured in 2- and 2½-in. chamber size. Firing a 2¾-in. shell in these firearms is dangerous. Other lengths are possible in gauge other than 12 gauge. If in doubt, check with a gunsmith. Actual shell length may vary slightly from these sized. Shell manufactures round off the sizes shown on the boxes.**

b. The following information is stamped on the barrel or action (see Figure 27) of most modern shotguns:

- Gauge
- Maximum shell length
- Type of choke

c. The gauge of a shotgun shell is printed on the base of the shell. The gauge and the shell length are also on the ammunition manufacturer's box. This information must be matched to the data stamp on the shotgun barrel prior to loading the firearm. If in doubt, check with a gunsmith or a gun shop.

d. If there is no data stamp, take the firearm to a gunsmith. The gunsmith can measure the firearm and give advice on proper ammunition.

⚠️ **Do not attempt to use longer ammunition than indicated on the barrel data stamp. If you do, the barrel might burst (see Figures 27 & 28).**

Figure 27. Shotgun shell head stamp, data stamp and ammunition box label

Data Stamp on Shotgun Barrel

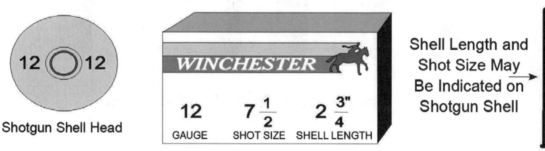

Shotgun Shell Head

Figure 28. Shell in chamber

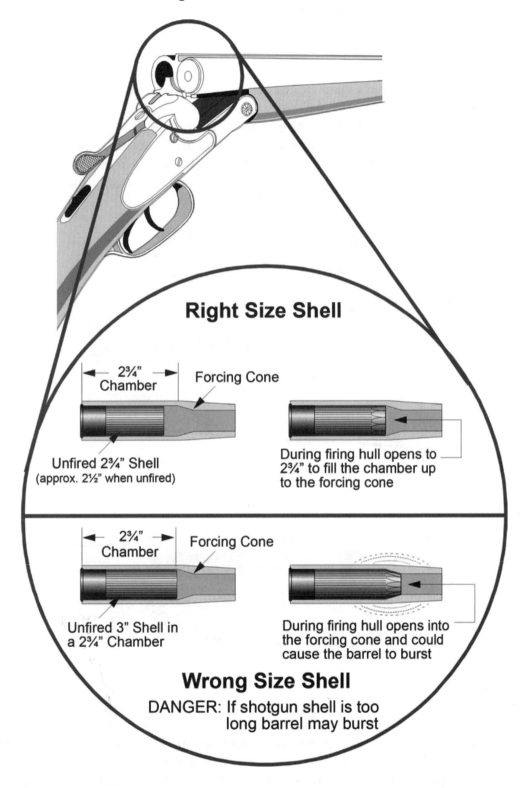

Right Size Shell

2¾" Chamber — Forcing Cone

Unfired 2¾" Shell
(approx. 2½" when unfired)

During firing hull opens to 2¾" to fill the chamber up to the forcing cone

2¾" Chamber — Forcing Cone

Unfired 3" Shell in a 2¾" Chamber

During firing hull opens into the forcing cone and could cause the barrel to burst

Wrong Size Shell

DANGER: If shotgun shell is too long barrel may burst

e. Chamber dimensions are given for a **fired** shell. Use the information on the box. If you measured an unfired shell, you might think a 3-in. shell is only 2¾" and have an accident.

⚠ **Serious accidents may occur when hunters or shooters load the wrong ammunition into their firearm. An easy mistake to make is loading and chambering a 20-gauge shotgun shell into a 12-gauge shotgun. The small shell will slide through the chamber and stick in the forcing cone. Users may then insert a 12-gauge shell behind the 20-gauge shell. When fired, the barrel may burst. Burst barrels scatter metal. People have been seriously injured or killed by this error.**

Figure 29. Exploded chamber

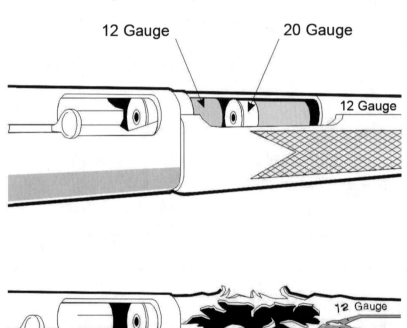

⚠ **For hunting, various provincial rules about shot and bullet size and materials exist. Your course instructor can provide more precise information. You can also check with your local hunting authority for exact regulations.**

3.9 Ballistics

a. Ballistics is the study of projectiles in flight, and what affects them.

b. Modern firearms can shoot a long way. For this reason, every shooter should understand ballistics. Shotguns can fire shot more than the length of a football field. Some rifles can fire bullets further than five kilometres.

c. Ballistics knowledge is also important because different ammunition has different penetrating effects. A projectile may not stop where you want it to.

d. Ballistics tables for ammunition supply the information to calculate the flight path and performance of cartridges.

e. You want to hunt or shoot safely. Therefore, you need to know how far your projectile will travel. That means you need to know the dangerous range (see Chart 3 – Dangerous range of rifle ammunition and Chart 4 – Dangerous range of shotgun ammunition).

 Be sure of your target and beyond. If there is any reason your shot may be unsafe, do not fire.

Chart 3. Dangerous range of rifle ammunition

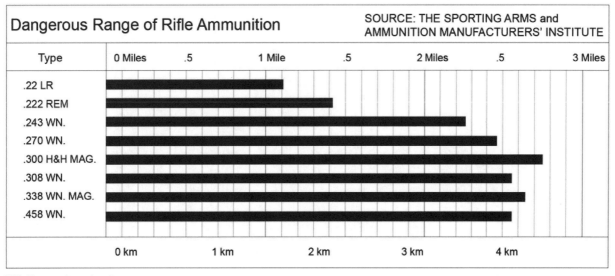

Range at sea level

Chart 4. Dangerous range of shotgun ammunition

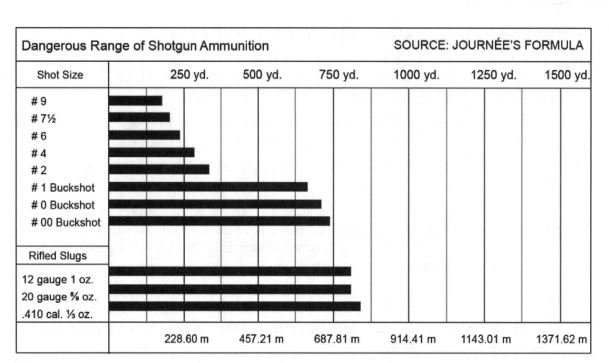

Dangerous Range of Shotgun Ammunition						SOURCE: JOURNÉE'S FORMULA	
Shot Size	250 yd.	500 yd.	750 yd.	1000 yd.	1250 yd.	1500 yd.
# 9						
# 7½						
# 6						
# 4						
# 2						
# 1 Buckshot						
# 0 Buckshot						
# 00 Buckshot						
Rifled Slugs						
12 gauge 1 oz.						
20 gauge ⅝ oz.						
.410 cal. ⅕ oz.						
	228.60 m	457.21 m	687.81 m	914.41 m	1143.01 m	1371.62 m

■ Range at sea level

NOTE: Steel, bismuth and tungsten-iron pellets of the same size have a shorter range.

3.10 Trajectory

a. Trajectory is the path a discharged shot or bullet takes during flight (see Figure 30). Several factors affect this path; they are gravity, air resistance, velocity, and mass.

- **Gravity** pulls the bullet down toward the ground as it is travelling forward. This results in a downward curved path.

- **Air resistance** holds back the passage of the bullet. This slows its flight.

- **Velocity** is the speed at which a bullet travels, in a given direction.

- **Mass** is the weight of the bullet.

b. The firearm muzzle must be raised from the horizontal position to make up for gravity. The trajectory of a projectile is slightly curved. It often crosses the line of sight twice on the way to a target.

Responsible shooters will follow the recommendations below:

- **Shoot only at targets within effective range.**
- **Consider how much farther the shot or bullet may travel beyond the target.**
- **Be prepared to be held responsible for where the bullet they shoot stops.**

Figure 30. Trajectory of a bullet

Trajectory or Path of a Bullet

Line of Sight

Exaggerated for Clarity

3.11 Hazards

a. The selection of the correct ammunition for the firearm is critical to safe operation but sometimes even the correct cartridge can fail to fire properly. Modern commercial ammunition is normally very reliable but there are several ways the cartridge may not fire.

- A **hang-fire** is a delayed fire in which the firing pin strikes the primer but it does not create enough flame to ignite the powder instantly. If the muzzle is not pointed in a safe direction when the cartridge eventually fires, it may result in an injury. If the cartridge is removed from the chamber and then discharges, the explosive rupture of the case may also cause injury. Muzzleloading firearms may also have a hang-fire.

- A **primer pop** (squib load) happens when the cartridge does not contain any gunpowder. The firearm will discharge the primer without the usual noise or recoil. This may have enough force to push the bullet out of the case, but the bullet may lodge in the barrel. If another bullet is fired, the barrel may rupture and cause possible injury.

- A **misfire** is a cartridge that does not fire. Misfired cartridges should not be reused in the firearm and must be disposed of properly. Muzzleloading firearms may also misfire.

 If the trigger is pulled and there is no noticeable discharge, wait 60 seconds while pointing the muzzle in a safe direction. If there is no hang-fire within 60 seconds, open the action and unload the firearm. PROVE the firearm safe to ensure there is no blockage lodged in the barrel.

3.12 Ammunition Precautions and Legislation

a. Explosives information is issued by Natural Resources Canada. It indicates that you may keep reasonable quantities of sporting ammunition on your property. "Reasonable" means quantities typically required for a rifle, handgun, or shotgun, or for part of a collection. This ammunition must be for your private use, not resale. Contact Natural Resources Canada for details. You must take every necessary precaution against accidents by adhering to the instructions below:

- Ammunition must be stored out of children's reach. It must be kept away from flammables.

- Ammunition for a non-restricted firearm may only be stored in a place where it is not within easy access to the firearm, unless the ammunition is stored, together with or separately from the firearm, in a securely locked container or receptacle that cannot be easily broken open or into.

- Ammunition for a non-restricted firearm must not be displayed with the firearm or be within easy access to the firearm from which it can be discharged.

- All ammunition should be stored in a cool, dry place. This will reduce the chance of corrosion or breakdown of the ammunition components that may cause the firearm to jam or misfire.

See Table 7 for a summary of ammunition safety points to remember.

 Keep in mind that storing ammunition in an unvented container may create an explosive hazard during a fire.

Table 7. Ammunition Safety Points to Remember

Ammunition Safety Points to Remember

- Carry ammunition only for the firearm you are using.

- Never experiment with unfamiliar ammunition.

- Using modern ammunition in old firearms may be hazardous.

- When a misfire occurs, slowly count to sixty while pointing the muzzle in a safe direction. Remove the cartridge following safe procedures. Then, carefully inspect the bore for obstructions.

- Never use old or corroded ammunition or reloading components.

- Never use military cartridges if you are not certain about their safe use.

- Never interchange smokeless powder and black powder. Use them only in firearms intended for their use.

- Store all ammunition so that unauthorized persons do not have access to it.

- Ammunition should never be displayed with a restricted firearm.

- Ammunition is most safely carried in its original container.

- When hand loading your own ammunition, be certain to strictly follow the procedures in the manuals about reloading ammunition. Treat primers with extra caution; they are explosive devices.

3.13 Review Questions

1. What safety precaution should be taken for a firearm that does not have a data stamp?

2. Describe four factors that affect trajectory.

3. What may occur if a 3-inch shell is used in a shotgun chambered for a 2¾" shell?

4. List the components of a cartridge and of a shell.

NOTES:

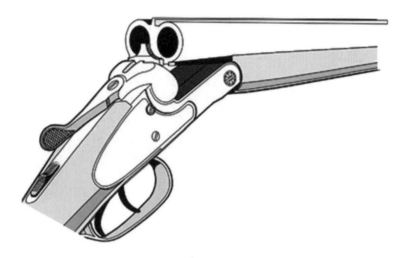

Section 4

OPERATING
FIREARM ACTIONS

4 - OPERATING FIREARM ACTIONS

4.0 Overview

a. To understand the safe use of firearms, you must become familiar with action types, how they work, and how to safely load and unload them.

b. This section defines the different types of firearms, various safeties and action releases, and explains the following procedures in detail:

- How to identify each type of action

- How to locate safeties (some actions will not open unless the safety is OFF)

- How to open actions and unload - **PROVE it safe**

- How to safely load each type of action, with the safety ON, whenever possible

 Always wear safety glasses and ear protection when loading and discharging firearms.

4.1 Muzzleloading and Antique Firearms

4.1.0 Overview

a. Muzzleloading muskets, pistols, rifles and shotguns are still in use today. However, most modern muzzleloaders are reproductions of older designs (see Figure 31).

b. This type of firearm is loaded through the muzzle. A measured amount of powder is poured through the muzzle into the barrel, followed by a patch and finally a lead ball, bullet or shot. A hole located at the rear of the barrel just above the trigger allows a flash or spark to enter the barrel through the priming port and ignite the powder, firing the charge.

c. With flintlock muzzleloaders, the igniting spark is the result of the flint, held by the cock, hitting the frizzen. On percussion muzzleloaders, the flash is produced by the hammer striking a percussion cap.

d. Muzzleloading firearms use black powder or black powder substitutes. Black powder is classified as an explosive and is easily ignited by heat, friction, static electricity or a sharp blow and must be handled with **extreme care.** It is strongly recommended that individuals interested in muzzleloading seek additional training from qualified specialists in the field.

 Older firearms should be inspected by a qualified gunsmith to be sure they can be fired safely.

Figure 31. Muzzleloader

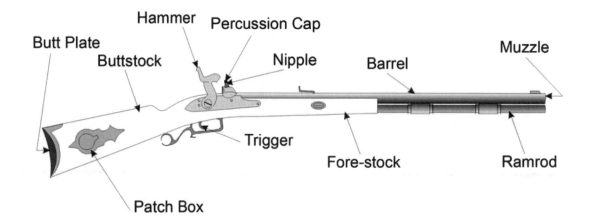

4.1.1 Loading Muzzleloaders

a. Today, most firearms for black powder use are reproductions of muzzleloaders. Older firearms may not be safe to fire and should be checked by a gunsmith before use.

b. If a muzzleloader is not primed to fire, it is safer to handle. To ensure that a muzzleloader is not primed to fire, do the following:

- Point the muzzle in the safest available direction and keep finger off the trigger and out of the trigger guard.

- Check that the hammer is **not** in full-cock position.

- Check for a percussion cap or see if the priming pan is primed.

- If the firearm is primed, remove cap or priming powder.

c. In addition, it is difficult to tell if there is already a charge loaded in the barrel of a muzzleloader. Experienced shooters mark the firearm's ramrod at a level that shows the bore depth when the bore is empty (see Figure 32). When the marked ramrod is inserted in the barrel, it shows whether or not the firearm is loaded.

Figure 32. Correctly marked ramrod

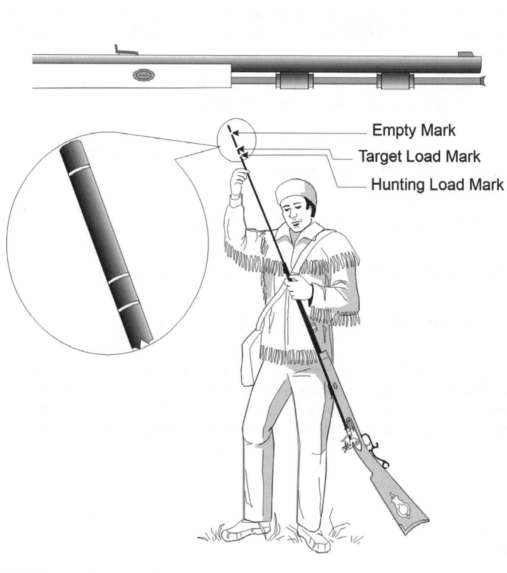

Empty Mark

Target Load Mark

Hunting Load Mark

PROVE the firearm safe.

⚠ **In the case of muzzleloading firearms that have a safety catch, activate the firearm before loading it. Before loading the firearm, use a cleaning rod with a fitted patch to check the gun bore and fire cap to ensure that nothing obstructs the chamber and gun bore. It is very important that exact loading and unloading procedures are followed when handling muzzleloaders (see Figures 33 & 34). Before attempting it, get the assistance of a qualified individual and carefully follow the instructions in your owner's guide.**

Figure 33. Loading a muzzleloader

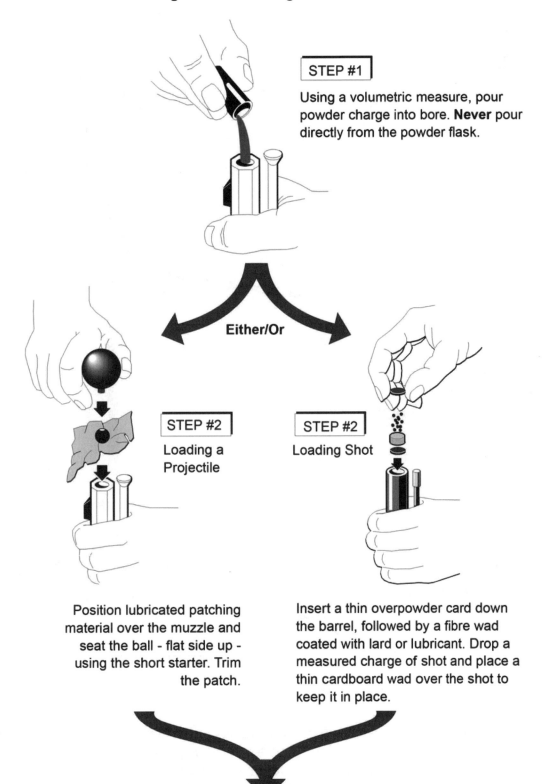

STEP #1

Using a volumetric measure, pour powder charge into bore. **Never** pour directly from the powder flask.

Either/Or

STEP #2

Loading a Projectile

STEP #2

Loading Shot

Position lubricated patching material over the muzzle and seat the ball - flat side up - using the short starter. Trim the patch.

Insert a thin overpowder card down the barrel, followed by a fibre wad coated with lard or lubricant. Drop a measured charge of shot and place a thin cardboard wad over the shot to keep it in place.

Continued

Figure 34. Loading a muzzleloader *(cont'd)*

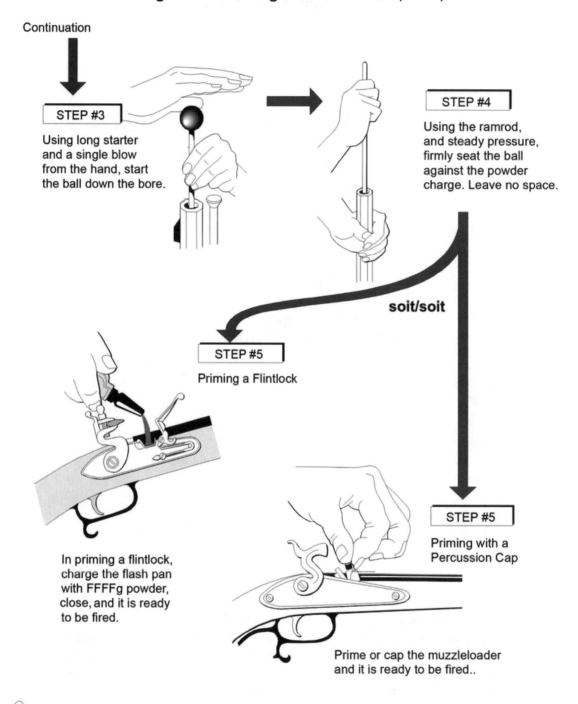

Continuation

STEP #3

Using long starter and a single blow from the hand, start the ball down the bore.

STEP #4

Using the ramrod, and steady pressure, firmly seat the ball against the powder charge. Leave no space.

soit/soit

STEP #5

Priming a Flintlock

In priming a flintlock, charge the flash pan with FFFFg powder, close, and it is ready to be fired.

STEP #5

Priming with a Percussion Cap

Prime or cap the muzzleloader and it is ready to be fired..

Never use smokeless powder in a muzzleloader. Never use black powder in a modern cartridge firearm not designed for it. Always use a volumetric measure to put powder into the muzzle; never pour directly from the main powder container. Under *safe-storage regulations*, black powder firearms are consideredloaded when powder and/or ball are in the barrel.

4.1.2 Do's and Don'ts of Muzzleloading

- **Do** have old muzzleloading firearms dismantled, examined and declared safe by a qualified gunsmith before using them.

- **Do** handle the muzzleloader with the same respect due all firearms.

- **Do** use ONLY black powder or black powder substitutes (i.e. Pyrodex) in your muzzleloader; never use smokeless powder.

- **Do** keep black powder far away from all cigarettes, matches/wicks or anything with an open flame, embers or anything that may cause sparks or heat.

- **Do** always use a powder measure to pour powder directly into the muzzle. Never use the powder horn or flask.

- **Do** carefully follow the manufacturer's recommendations for maximum powder charge.

- **Do** mark your ramrod to indicate when the barrel is empty and when it is loaded.

- **Do** wipe the bore clean of oil and excess grease **before** you load.

- **Do** make sure the ball or bullet is seated firmly on the powder charge.

- **Do** treat a misfire as a hang-fire that could fire at any second. Wait at least 60 seconds with the firearm pointed in a safe direction.

- **Do** wear safety glasses and hearing protection.

- **Do** reseat your second charge after firing and reloading a single barrel on a multiple-barrel black powder firearm. Recoil can move the charge forward.

- **Don't** carry or handle a muzzleloading firearm with the hammer at full cock and primed unless you are ready to fire.

- **Don't** lean over or stand in front of the muzzle at any time.

- **Don't** load one barrel of a double-barrelled-muzzleloading shotgun unless the percussion cap on the nipple of the other barrel has been removed.

- **Don't** store a muzzleloader with powder in it.

However, loaded muzzleloading firearms **may** be carried from one hunting ground to another if the firing cap or flint is removed, subject to provincial/territorial regulations.

⚠ **Black powder is also used in some metallic cartridges for firearms specifically designed for their use. Care should be taken. Although they have the same name as a modern smokeless cartridge, they may not be interchangeable. Never interchange smokeless powder and black powder. Use them only in firearms intended for their use.**

4.2 Action Types

a. Firearms are generally classified by their type of action. There are six basic types (see Figure 35):

1. A **hinge (or break) action** opens near the breech and is usually single or double barrelled.

2. A **bolt action i**s similar to a door bolt and can be single or multiple shot.

3. A **lever action** has a metal handle just behind the trigger that opens the action. It can be single or multiple shot.

4. A **pump action** works by pumping the fore-end of the stock back and forth and is normally multiple shot.

5. A **semi-automatic action** extracts and ejects empty casings and inserts another cartridge in the chamber automatically.

6. A **revolving action** is used in some handguns. It has several chambers in a rotating cylinder and can contain one cartridge in each chamber. Revolvers are manufactured as non-swing-out cylinder, swing-out cylinder or top break.

Figure 35. Types of actions

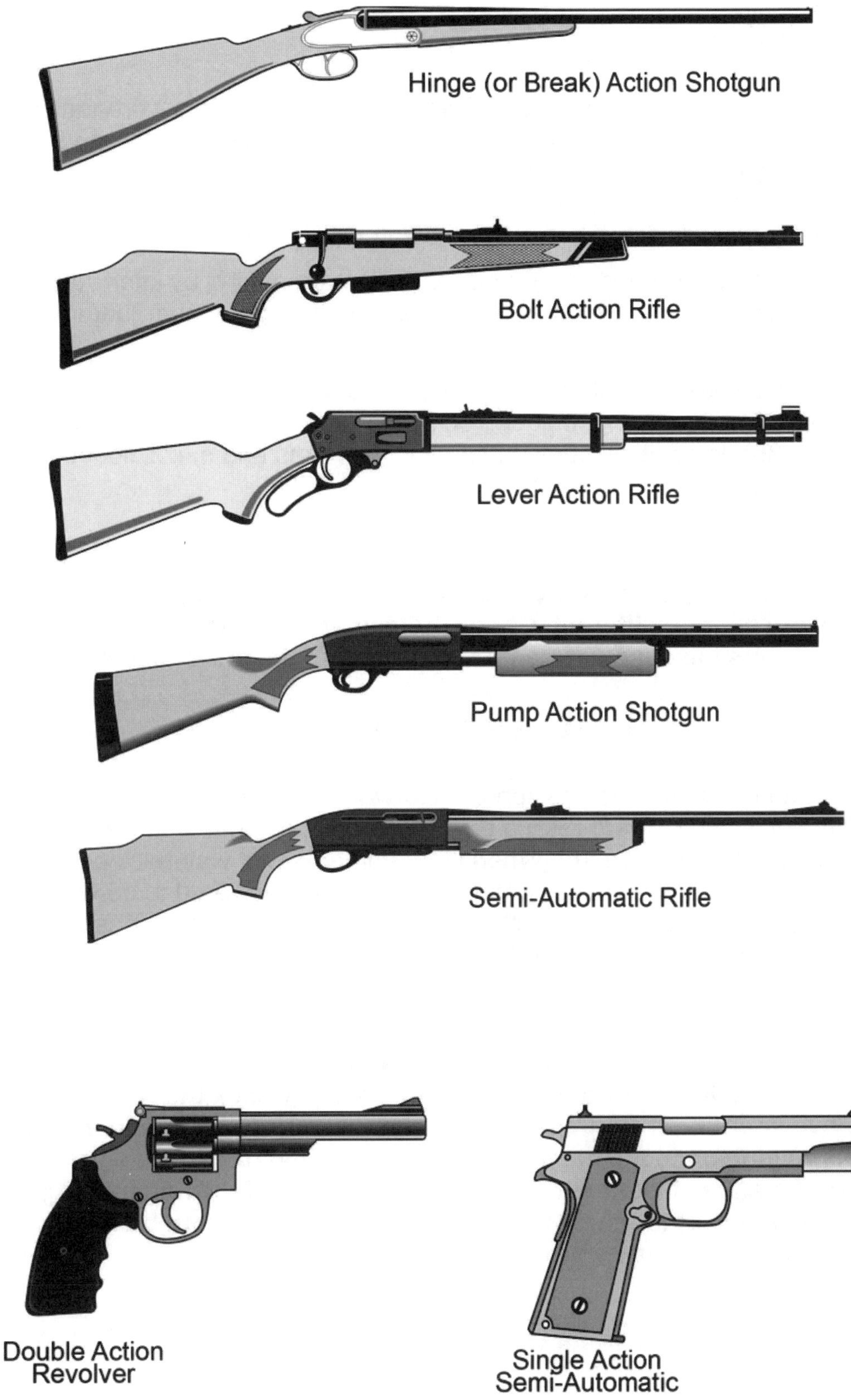

Hinge (or Break) Action Shotgun

Bolt Action Rifle

Lever Action Rifle

Pump Action Shotgun

Semi-Automatic Rifle

Double Action
Revolver

Single Action
Semi-Automatic

4.3 Safeties

4.3.0 Overview

a. A mechanical device known as a **safety** is included on most firearms to reduce the chances of accidental firing. However, mechanical devices can fail. A hard blow may cause some firearms to fire even with the safety **ON**. Therefore, safe handling of a firearm by the person holding it will always be the most important firearm safety device. Always use the safety, but never rely on it to prevent firing.

b. The safety is designed to prevent the firearm from firing by interrupting the firing sequence. The safety blocks one or more of the trigger, sear, hammer or firing pin.

c. Common types of safeties on non-restricted firearms are the slide/tang, pivot/lever/rocker, wing, trigger block/lever, and cross-bolt or button safety (see Figure 36). In addition, some lever action firearms and muzzleloaders use a half-cock safety.

Never rely on a safety to prevent accidental firing. A safety can fail. All safeties are slightly different. Check the owner's manual. Different manufacturers may use different terminology to describe their safeties.

4.3.1 Hammer on Half-Cock Notch

a. The hammer has three positions: full forward, half cock, and full cock. When the hammer is fully forward resting on the firing pin, a sudden blow on the hammer may discharge the firearm. When the hammer is part-way-back or in half-cock position, on firearms so designed, the safety is considered to be **ON**. When the hammer is all the way back on such firearms, it is in full-cock position and the safety is considered to be **OFF.**

The presence of a half cock on a firearm does not guarantee it is a safety. Some firearms do not use it as a safety. Check the owner's manual. Remove your finger from the trigger when lowering the hammer to the half-cock position once the hammer starts to go forward. This will re-engage any automatic safety linked to the trigger. Be very careful when moving the hammer in any of the three positions as it could slip from beneath your thumb and fire the cartridge.

Figure 36. Various types of safeties and action releases

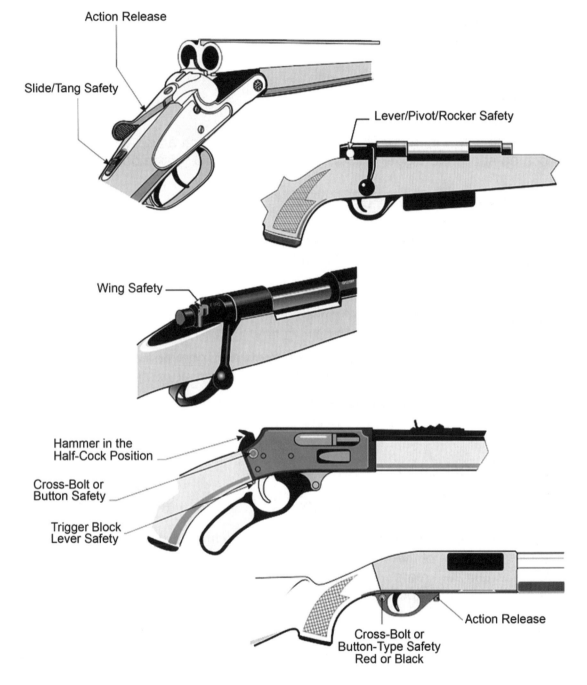

4.3.2 Slide/Tang

a. This safety is common on shotguns and rifles. It is usually on the right side of the receiver on rifles, and the top of the receiver on shotguns. It blocks the firing mechanism. Some modern lever actions also have slide or button type safeties located in the action area.

4.3.3 Pivot/Lever/Rocker

a. This safety is commonly found on modern firearms as well as older military firearms. It is often located above the trigger area on the left or right side of the bolt.

4.3.4 Wing

a. The wing safety is frequently used on the bolt of a bolt action firearm. It is often located above the trigger area on the left or right side of the bolt.

4.3.5 Trigger Block/Lever

a. This safety is used on some lever action firearms. It is a mechanism that ensures the lever action firearm will not fire unless the lever action is pressed firmly against the stock.

4.3.6 Cross-Bolt Safety

a. The cross-bolt is a push-button type of safety. It is common on many types of firearms. It works by blocking the trigger mechanism or hammer.

b. The safety position can be indicated in several ways as follows:

- **Safe** and **Fire**

- **ON** and **OFF** switch

- **Red**, which means that the safety is **OFF**, and the firearm can be fired.

c. However, there is no standard rule for indicating the safety position, and sometimes none of the above positions can be found on the firearm. If so, check to be certain the firearm is unloaded and pointing in a safe direction **BEFORE** checking the safety operation.

 Before loading any firearm, determine the ON position of the safety.

4.4 Action Releases

a. Most firearms have some type of mechanism that must be moved to allow an action to be opened or closed. The location of the action release mechanism depends on the make and model of the firearm (see Figure 36 in section 4.3.1).

⚠ **Do not touch any firearm unless you know how to handle it safely. Get help from the owner's manual, or a person who knows that firearm well.**

4.5 General Loading and Unloading Procedures

4.5.0 Overview

a. Before attempting to unload a firearm, first follow the **Vital Four ACTS** in Table 8 below.

Table 8. The Vital Four ACTS of Firearm Safety

	The Vital Four ACTS of Firearm Safety
☞	**A**ssume every firearm is loaded. • Regard any firearm as a potential danger.
☞	**C**ontrol the muzzle direction at all times. • Identify the safest available muzzle direction. • Keep the firearm pointed in the safest available direction. • The muzzle of a firearm should not be pointed towards yourself or any other person.
☞	**T**rigger finger must be kept off the trigger and out of the trigger guard. • Resist the temptation to put your finger on the trigger or inside the trigger guard when you pick up a firearm. • Accidental discharge is far more likely to occur if your finger is on the trigger or inside the trigger guard.
☞	**S**ee that the firearm is unloaded - PROVE it safe. • Do not handle the firearm unless you can properly **PROVE** it safely. • Check to see that both chamber and magazine are empty. Do this every time you handle a firearm, for any reason. • Pass or accept only open and unloaded firearms. This is an important habit to develop.

4.5.1 Unloading Procedures - PROVE Safe

a. **PROVE** is an acronym, or memory aid, that stands for the five steps required to ensure a firearm unloaded and safe. The five steps are: **P**oint, **R**emove, **O**bserve, **V**erify and **E**xamine. These procedures must be followed to safely unload any firearm.

1. **P**oint the firearm in the safest available direction throughout the unloading procedure.

   - Make sure that nothing touches the trigger throughout this procedure.
   - Put the safety **ON**, if it can be left on during the unloading process.

2. **R**emove all ammunition as follows:

   - If the firearm is a semi-automatic with a detachable magazine, remove the magazine from the firearm first. Open the action to remove any ammunition from the chamber. (This prevents a semi-automatic from chambering another cartridge if the action closes.)

   - For virtually all other actions, open the action to remove any ammunition from the chamber(s). Remove any magazine and all other ammunition from the firearm. (The danger of a manual action closing on its own is much lower than a semi-automatic.)

   - Leave the action open.

3. **O**bserve the chamber(s) to confirm that there is no ammunition or empty casing(s).

4. **V**erify by inspecting the feeding path to make sure it is empty of ammunition, empty casings, or foreign objects. Make certain you see or feel the follower, if one is present.

5. **E**xamine the bore (s) every time you pick up a firearm for lubricant, rust, or obstructions.

The firearm is now unloaded and safe until it leaves the direct control of the person who unloaded and PROVEd it safe.

4.5.2 Checking the Barrel for Obstructions

a. In all of the following loading procedures, **always check the barrel and chamber for obstructions before loading.** Whenever possible, this should be done by looking through the barrel from the BACK or breech end. If you cannot, be very certain the firearm is unloaded and the action is open and chamber empty BEFORE looking down the barrel from the muzzle end. Some shooters prefer to use a bore light inspection aid or run a rod with a patch through the barrel before loading, rather than looking down the barrel. Use normal cleaning procedures to remove an obstruction, or take the firearm to an expert.

 Unless the patch fills the bore completely, obstructions may not be detected. Only load a firearm when you intend to use it, and only in an area where it can be safely and legally discharged.

4.5.3 Loading Procedure

1. Prepare the firearm for loading by going through the complete unloading procedure - **PROVE it safe.**

2. Clear any obstructions from the chamber(s) and bore(s). Clean if required.

3. Point the firearm in the safest available direction throughout the loading and chambering procedure.

4. Make sure that nothing touches the trigger throughout this process.

5. Put the safety ON, if it can be left on during the loading process.

6. Where possible, with the action open, select and load the correct ammunition by matching the data stamp on the firearm with the head stamp on the cartridge/shell or ammunition box.

7. Close the action.

8. Put the safety ON, if it is not already on.

The firearm is now loaded and ready for use. It requires continuous care and attention until it is unloaded.

 Always be sure of your target and beyond.

4.6 Loading and Unloading the Most Common Action Types

a. All firearms have their own unique aspects. One of the best ways to discover the detailed methods for unloading and loading your particular firearm is to study the owner's manual. The steps outlined in this section are not meant to replace a full understanding of a given firearm owner's manual.

b. The following information is an introduction to the most common actions. The general procedure does not change, but the details can vary significantly.

 All firearms may not be able to be handled safely by all persons, i.e. grip is too large, the slide lock is out of reach, etc. Do not attempt to handle any firearm that you are uncomfortable handling. To ensure proper fit of any firearm, seek the assistance of a qualified individual. Before attempting to unload a firearm, follow the Vital Four ACTS.

4.7 Hinge (or Break) Action: Single or Multiple Barrels

4.7.1 Unloading Procedure - PROVE Safe

a. The hinge (or break) action firearm opens or "breaks" near the breech like the movement of a door hinge. The **safety mechanism** is usually located on top of the action above the trigger area. It is often a slide/tang safety or exposed hammer which must be completely down or on half cock to be safe.

1. **P**oint the firearm in the safest available direction throughout the unloading procedure.

   • Make sure that nothing touches the trigger throughout this procedure.

   • Put the safety ON, if it can be left on during the unloading process.

2. **R**emove all ammunition as follows:

   • Move the action release to open the action. If the action release will not move, the safety may need to be moved to the OFF position.

   • Open the action by hinging the barrel (normally it drops downward). This should partly extract or eject any ammunition or empty casing/hull from the chamber(s). If not ejected, remove them by hand.

   • Leave the action open.

3. **O**bserve the chamber(s) to confirm that there is no ammunition or empty casing(s)/hull(s).

4. **V**erify by inspecting the feeding path to make sure it is empty of ammunition, empty casings/hulls, or foreign objects.

5. **E**xamine the bore(s) every time you pick up a firearm for lubricant, rust, or obstructions.

The firearm is now unloaded and safe until it leaves the direct control of the person who unloaded and PROVEd it safe.

Figure 37. Hinge (or break) action

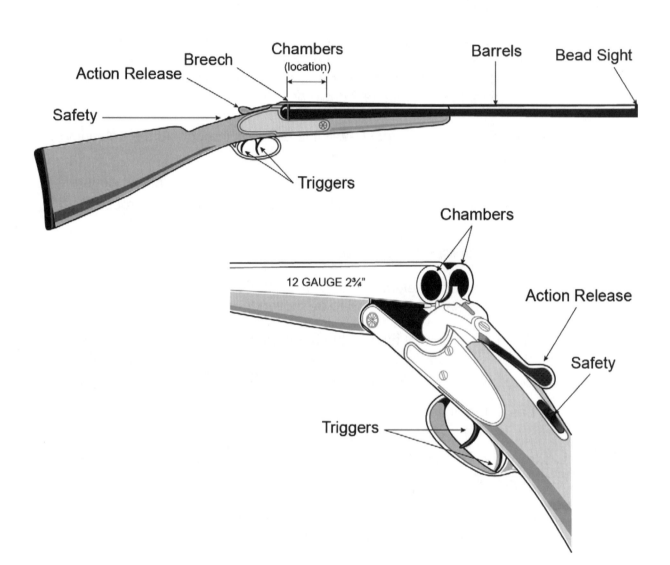

⚠️ Only load a firearm when you intend to use it, and only in an area where it can be safely and legally discharged.

4.7.2 Loading Procedure

1. Prepare the firearm for loading by going through the complete unloading procedure - **PROVE it safe**.

2. Clear any obstructions from the chamber(s) and bore(s). Clean if required.

3. Point the firearm in the safest available direction throughout the loading and chambering procedure.

4. Make sure that nothing touches the trigger throughout this process.

5. Put the safety **ON**, if it can be left on during the loading process.

6. Select and place the correct ammunition into the chamber(s) by matching the data stamp on the firearm with the head stamp on the cartridge/casing or ammunition box.

7. Close the action (typically by snapping it closed with a firm action), locking the cartridge(s)/shell (s) into the chamber(s).

8. Put the safety **ON**, if it is not already on.

The firearm is now loaded and ready for use. It requires continuous care and attention until it is unloaded.

Always be sure of your target and beyond.

4.8 Single Shot

4.8.0 Overview

a. A bolt action firearm operates something like a door bolt. This action is very strong and is most often used on rifles.

b. The **safety mechanism** is usually located on top of the action above the trigger area on the left or right side of the bolt. This is often a lever safety but can also be a slide/tang located directly behind the bolt (see Figures 38 and 39).

Figure 38. Bolt action

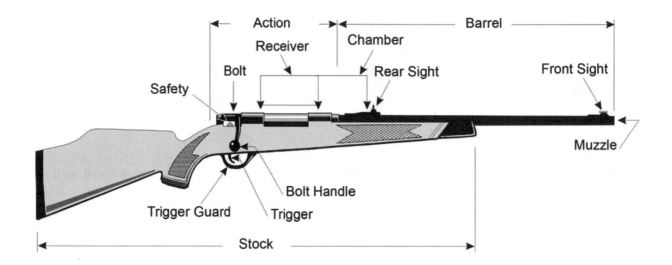

Figure 39. Single-shot rifle utilizing bolt action to eject empty casing

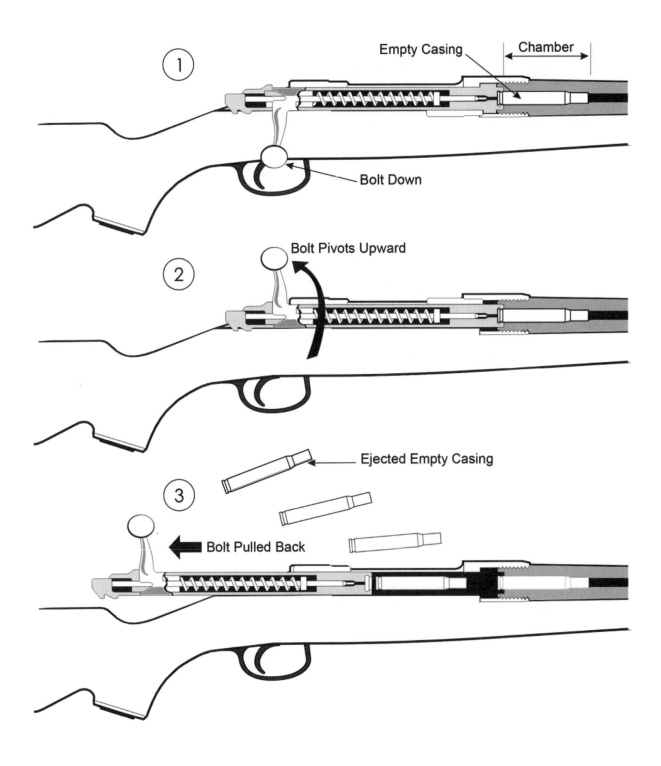

4.8.1 Single Shot Unloading Procedure - PROVE Safe

> ⚠ **Before attempting to unload a firearm, follow the Vital Four ACTS.**

1. **P**oint the firearm in the safest available direction throughout the unloading procedure.

   - Make sure that nothing touches the trigger throughout this procedure.

   - Put the safety **ON**, if it can be left on during the unloading process.

2. **R**emove all ammunition as follows:

   - Open the action by moving the bolt handle (typically by lifting and pulling to the rear). This should extract and eject any ammunition or empty casing/hull from the chamber. If not ejected, remove it by hand.

   - Leave the action open.

3. **O**bserve the chamber to confirm that there is no ammunition or empty casing/hull.

4. **V**erify by inspecting the feeding path to make sure it is empty of ammunition, empty casings/hulls, or foreign objects.

5. **E**xamine the bore every time you pick up a firearm for lubricant, rust, or obstructions.

The firearm is now unloaded and safe until it leaves the direct control of the person who unloaded and PROVEd it safe.

4.8.2 Single Shot Loading Procedure

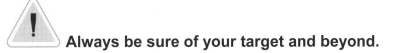 **Only load a firearm when you intend to use it, and only in an area where it can be safely and legally discharged.**

1. Prepare the firearm for loading by going through the complete unloading procedure - **PROVE it safe**.

2. Clear any obstruction from the chamber and bore. Clean if required.

3. Point the firearm in the safest available direction throughout the loading and chambering procedure.

4. Make sure that nothing touches the trigger throughout this process.

5. Put the safety **ON,** if it can be left on during the loading process.

6. Where possible, with the action open, select and place the correct ammunition into the chamber by matching the data stamp on the firearm with the head stamp on the cartridge/shell or ammunition box.

7. Place the ammunition in the chamber or feeding tray.

8. Close the actions by moving the bolt handle forward and down, locking the cartridge into the chamber.

9. Put the safety **ON**, if it is not already on.

The firearm is now loaded and ready for use. It requires continuous care and attention until it is unloaded.

Always be sure of your target and beyond.

4.9 Operating Repeating Firearms

4.9.0 Overview

a. Many firearms are repeaters. Although they have only one chamber, they can be fired several times in a row because they hold more than one cartridge or shell. Some kind of hand movement must be made by the shooter to load another cartridge into the firing position. The most common repeating firearms include the following:

- Bolt action repeater

- Lever action

- Pump action

- Semi-automatic

- Revolver

b. The extra ammunition in a repeating firearm is usually contained in some kind of magazine. Magazines are located in different places depending on the make, model and action of the firearm. There are two common types of magazines as follows:

- Box-type

- Tubular-type

4.9.1 Box-Type Magazines

a. The usual location of a **box-type magazine** is shown in Figure 40. Some box-type magazines may be removed by depressing a button or latch. Some are not removable.

Figure 40. Box-type magazines

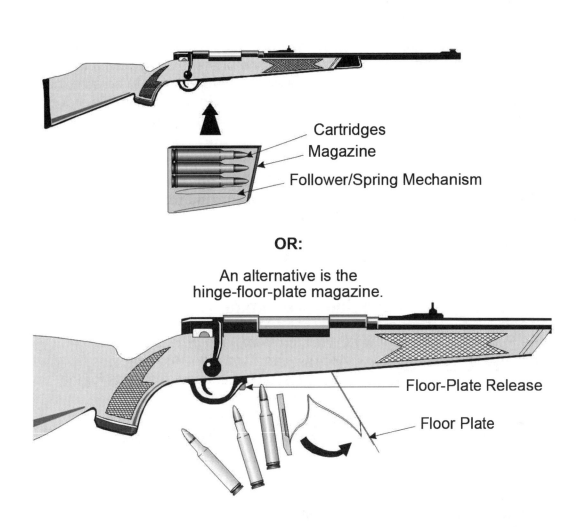

Cartridges
Magazine
Follower/Spring Mechanism

OR:

An alternative is the
hinge-floor-plate magazine.

Floor-Plate Release

Floor Plate

4.9.2 Tubular-Type Magazines

a. The tubular-type magazine is usually found in one of two locations:

- Under the barrel; or

- In the stock.

b. Many tubular magazines consist of a removable-inner magazine tube (which should be removed when unloading the firearm). In others, there is only one tube or the inner tube cannot be removed.

c. To unload tubular magazines, remove the inside tube and let the ammunition drop out of the end of the fixed-tubular magazine or the loading port. If the inner tube is not removable, close and open the action several times to be sure there are no ammunition in the magazine. Take extra care in performing this procedure because when doing so, the firearm is in the ready-to-fire position.

 Ammunition could hang-up in the tubular magazine, due to dirt, rust or dents. Always be sure you can feel or see the magazine follower to confirm that all the ammunition is out (see Figure 41).

Table 9. Magazine-Size Limits

Magazine-Size Limits
Part 4 of the *Regulations Prescribing Certain Firearms and other Weapons, Components, and Parts of Weapons, Accessories, Cartridge Magazines, Ammunition and Projectiles as Prohibited or Restricted* sets out the limits for the number of cartridges permitted for different types of magazines.
For example, centre-fire semi-automatic rifles and shotguns including "grandfathered" full-automatics and converted full-automatics—5-shot magazines.

d. These restrictions do not apply to rim-fire rifles, M-1 Garand rifles and other rare and historically valuable magazines that have been specifically exempt, plus non semi-automatic rifles (pump, lever, or bolt action). Prior to July 1993, owners of large-capacity cartridge magazines that were affected by the limits were able to retain them if they had been properly modified to comply with the limits.

Using pointed centre-fire ammunition in a tubular magazine is hazardous. If jarred, the point on one of the cartridges may detonate the primer of the one in front of it.

Figure 41. Tubular-type magazines

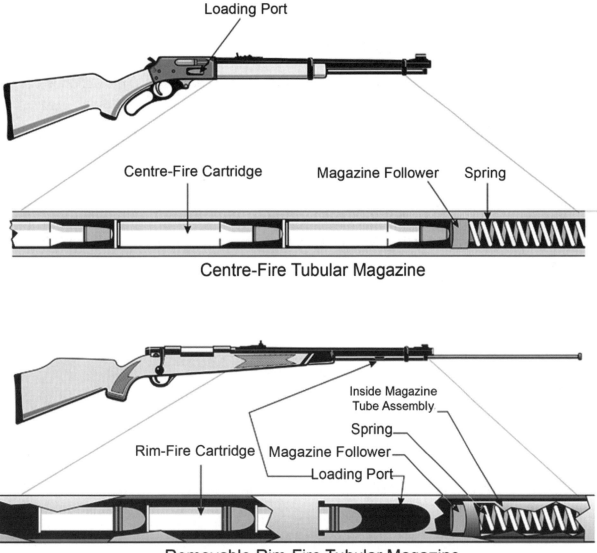

Loading Port

Centre-Fire Cartridge   Magazine Follower   Spring

Centre-Fire Tubular Magazine

Inside Magazine Tube Assembly

Spring

Rim-Fire Cartridge   Magazine Follower

Loading Port

Removable Rim-Fire Tubular Magazine

4.10 Bolt Action Repeaters

4.10.0 Overview

a. Federal, provincial and territorial laws may affect the number of cartridges you are allowed to have in a magazine while hunting. Consult your course instructor or your provincial/territorial hunting authority.

b. A bolt action firearm operates in a similar way to a door bolt. This action is very strong and is most often used on rifles

c. The **safety mechanism** is usually located on top of the action above the trigger area on the left or right side of the bolt. This is often a lever type safety but can also be a slide/tang located directly behind the bolt (see Figure 42).

Before attempting to unload a firearm, follow the Vital Four ACTS.

Figure 42. Bolt action repeater

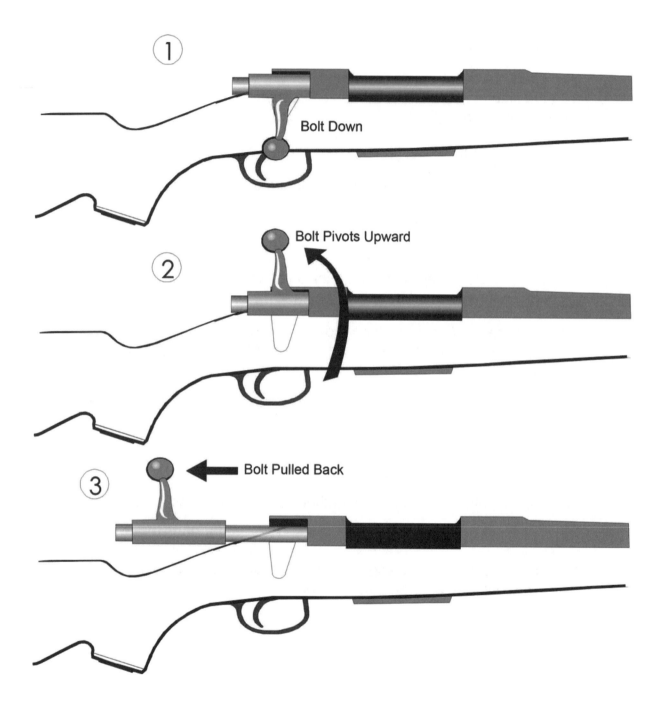

4.10.1 Unloading Procedure - PROVE Safe

Before attempting to unload a firearm, follow the Vital Four ACTS.

1. **P**oint the firearm in the safest available direction throughout the unloading procedure.

    -   Make sure that nothing touches the trigger throughout this procedure.

    -   Put the safety **ON**, if it can be left on during the unloading process.

2. **R**emove all ammunition as follows:

    -   Open the action by moving the bolt handle (typically up and to the rear). This should extract and eject any ammunition or empty casing/hull from the chamber. If not ejected, remove it by hand.

    -   If the magazine (inner tubular or box) is removable, remove the magazine. Remove any ammunition using gravity to make it fall out (typically from the front of the open end of the tubular magazine.)

    -   If ammunition cannot be removed in any other way, cycle all the cartridges through the chamber to get them out.

    -   Leave the action open.

3. **O**bserve the chamber to confirm that there is no ammunition or empty casing/hull.

4. **V**erify by inspecting the feeding path to make sure it is empty of ammunition, empty casings/hulls, or foreign objects. Make certain you see or feel the follower if one is present.

5. **E**xamine the bore every time you pick up a firearm for lubricant, rust, or obstructions.

The firearm is now unloaded and safe until it leaves the direct control of the person who unloaded and PROVEd it safe.

4.10.2 Loading Procedure

⚠️ **Only load a firearm when you intend to use it, and only in an area where it can be safely and legally discharged.**

1. Prepare the firearm for loading by going through the complete unloading procedure - **PROVE it safe.**

2. Clear any obstruction from the chamber and bore. Clean if required.

3. Point the firearm in the safest available direction throughout the loading and chambering procedure.

4. Make sure that nothing touches the trigger throughout this process.

5. Put the safety **ON**, if it can be left on during the loading process.

6. On some firearms, you must release the spring tension on the follower at this point.

7. Select and place the correct ammunition into the magazine by matching the data stamp on the firearm with the head stamp on the cartridge or ammunition box.

8. Reapply spring tension to the follower or insert the magazine, if necessary.

9. Close the action by moving the bolt handle (typically forward and downward) feeding and locking a cartridge into the chamber.

10. Put the safety **ON,** if it is not already on.

The firearm is now loaded and ready for use. It requires continuous care and attention until it is unloaded.

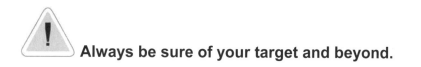 **Always be sure of your target and beyond.**

4.11 Lever Action Repeaters

4.11.0 Overview

a. A lever action firearm has a metal handle located just behind the trigger (see Figure 43). This action is most often used on rifles.

b. In most cases, the **safety mechanism** is an exposed hammer. The hammer has three positions—forward, half cock and full cock. When the hammer is in half-cock position, the safety is considered to be **ON**. When the hammer is all-the-way-back, it is in full-cock position and the safety is considered to be **OFF**. However, when the hammer is fully forward resting on the firing pin, a sudden blow on the hammer can discharge the firearm.

c. This type of lever action often will not fire unless the lever is fully squeezed against the stock depressing the trigger-block safety.

d. Some modern lever action firearms also have slide/tang or cross-bolt/button safeties located in the action area.

Figure 43. Lever action

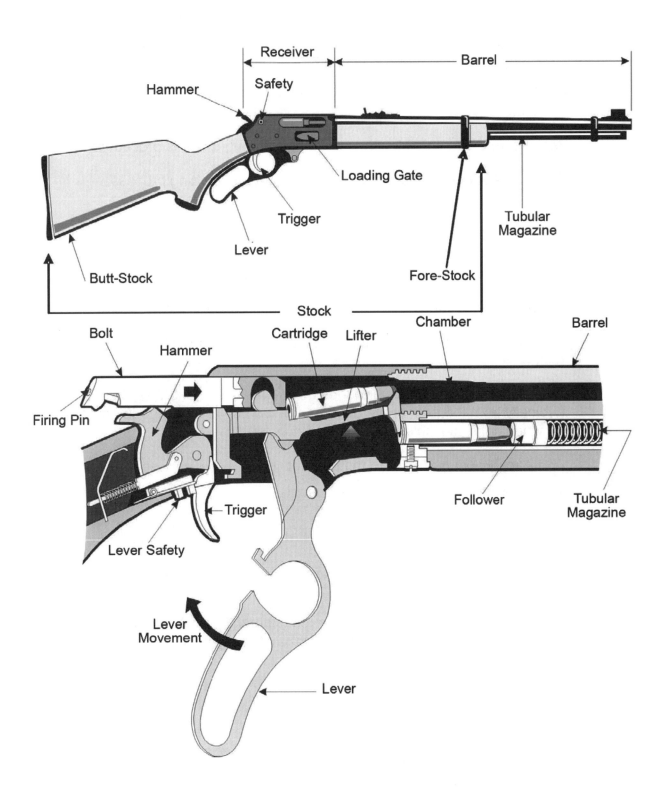

4.11.1 Unloading Procedure - PROVE Safe

 **Before attempting to unload a firearm, follow the Vital Four ACTS.**

1. **P**oint the firearm in the safest available direction throughout the unloading procedure.

   • Make sure that nothing touches the trigger throughout this procedure.

   • Put the safety **ON**, if it can be left on during the unloading process.

2. **R**emove all cartridges as follows:

   • Open the action by moving the lever downward. This should extract and eject any cartridge or empty casing from the chamber.

   • If the magazine (inner tubular or box) is removable, remove the magazine.

   • If it cannot be removed, and if spring tension to the follower can be released, release it.

   • If applicable, remove any cartridges using gravity to make them fall out (typically from the front of the open end of the box or inner-tubular magazine or, when not removable, from the loading port), then

      • reapply spring tension to the follower, and

      • cycle the action (close and re-open it).

   • Leave the action open.

3. **O**bserve the chamber to confirm that there is no cartridge or empty casing/hull.

4. **V**erify by inspecting the feeding path to make sure it is empty of cartridges, empty casings/hulls, or foreign objects. Make certain you see or feel the follower if one is present.

5. **E**xamine the bore for lubricant, rust, or obstructions.

The firearm is now unloaded and safe until it leaves the direct control of the person who unloaded and PROVEd it safe.

4.11.2 Loading Procedure

1. Prepare the firearm for loading by going through the complete unloading procedure - **PROVE it safe**.

2. Clear any obstructions from the chamber and bore. Clean if required.

3. Point the firearm in the safest available direction throughout the loading and chambering procedure.

4. Make sure that nothing touches the trigger throughout this process.

5. Put the safety **ON,** if it can be left on during the loading process.

6. Where possible, with action open, select the correct cartridge by matching the data stamp on the firearm with the head stamp on the cartridge or the ammunition box and insert into the magazine.

7. Insert cartridge through the loading gate into the magazine.

8. Close the action by moving the lever, feeding and locking a cartridge into the chamber.

9. Put the safety **ON**, if it is not already on.

The firearm is now loaded and ready for use. It requires continuous care and attention until it is unloaded.

⚠ **Only load a firearm when you intend to use it, and only in an area where it can be safely and legally discharged. Always be sure of your target and beyond.**

4.12 Pump Action Repeaters

4.12.0 Overview

a. The pump action firearm is sometimes called the slide or trombone action because the fore-end of the stock is pumped back and forth to operate the action. It permits rapid reloading with a simple movement of the firearm supporting hand without moving the muzzle away from the target. This action is most commonly used on shotguns. Either a box or a tubular magazine may be used.

b. The **safety mechanism** on most modern pump actions is either a slide/tang or cross-bolt/button safety located in the action area. The button is usually at the front or rear of the trigger guard. The slide/tang is frequently on top of the action. The action release is also found at the trigger guard (see Figure 44).

Figure 44. Pump action

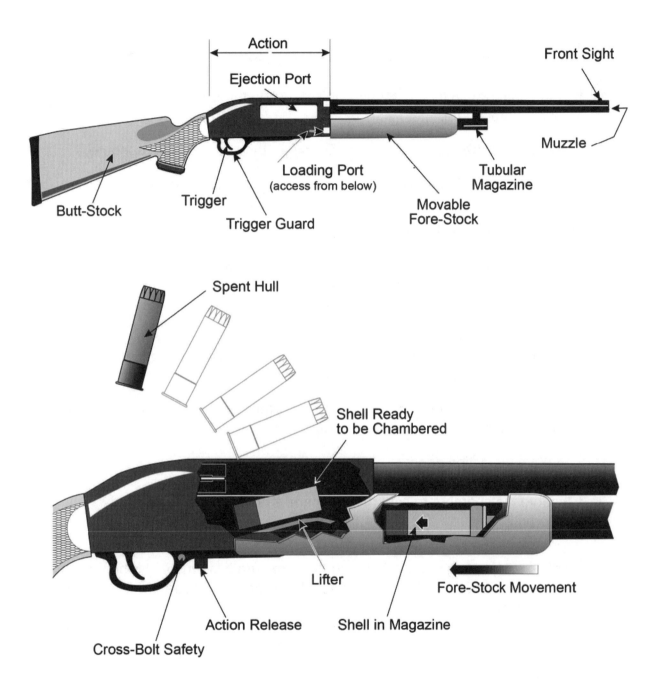

4.12.1 Unloading Procedure - PROVE Safe

Before attempting to unload a firearm, follow the Vital Four ACTS.

1. **P**oint the firearm in the safest available direction throughout the unloading procedure.

   - Make sure that nothing touches the trigger throughout this procedure.

   - Put the safety **ON,** if it can be left on during the unloading process.

2. **R**emove all ammunition as follows:

   - Open the action by depressing the action release and sliding the fore-stock to the rear. This should extract and eject any ammunition or empty casing/hull from the chamber. If not ejected, remove it by hand.

   - If the magazine (inner tubular or box) is removable, remove the magazine. Remove any ammunition using gravity to make it fall out (typically from the front of the open end of the tubular magazine.)

   - If ammunition cannot be removed in any other way, cycle all the cartridges through the chamber to get them out.

   - Leave the action open.

3. **O**bserve the chamber to confirm that there is no ammunition or empty casing/hull.

4. **V**erify by inspecting the feeding path to make sure it is empty of ammunition, empty casings/hulls, or foreign objects. Make certain you see or feel the follower if one is present.

5. **E**xamine the bore every time you pick up a firearm for lubricant, rust, or obstructions.

The firearm is now unloaded and safe until it leaves the direct control of the person who unloaded and PROVEd it safe.

4.12.2 Loading Procedure

⚠ **Only load a firearm when you intend to use it, and only in an area where it can be safely and legally discharged.**

1. Prepare the firearm for loading by going through the complete unloading procedure - **PROVE it safe**.

2. Clear any obstructions from the chamber and bore. Clean if required.

3. Point the firearm in the safest available direction throughout the loading and chambering procedure.

4. Make sure that nothing touches the trigger throughout this process.

5. Put the safety **ON**, if it can be left on during the loading process.

6. Move the fore-stock to the forward position to close the action.

7. Select and place the correct ammunition into the magazine by matching the data stamp on the firearm with the head stamp on the cartridge/shell or ammunition box.

8. Cycle the action moving a cartridge from the magazine into the chamber.

9. Put the safety **ON**, if it is not already on.

The firearm is now loaded and ready for use. It requires continuous care and attention until it is unloaded.

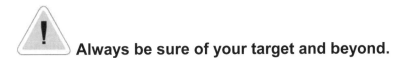 **Always be sure of your target and beyond.**

4.13 Semi-Automatic Action Repeaters

4.13.0 Overview

a. This action can be found on rifles, shotguns and handguns.

b. With each pull of the trigger, the semi-automatic action uses part of the energy of the expanding gas from the burning powder to extract the empty cartridge case and to reload the chamber. In other words, no hand movement is needed to load another cartridge into the firing position; each time a cartridge is fired, another is loaded into the chamber (see Figure 45).

c. Semi-automatic safeties vary considerably. The safety mechanisms commonly used are cross-bolt/button and slide/tang types. Occasionally, internal safeties such as a magazine disconnect are used. These prevent the firearm from firing when the magazine is not in place.

Figure 45. Firing sequence of a semi-automatic rifle

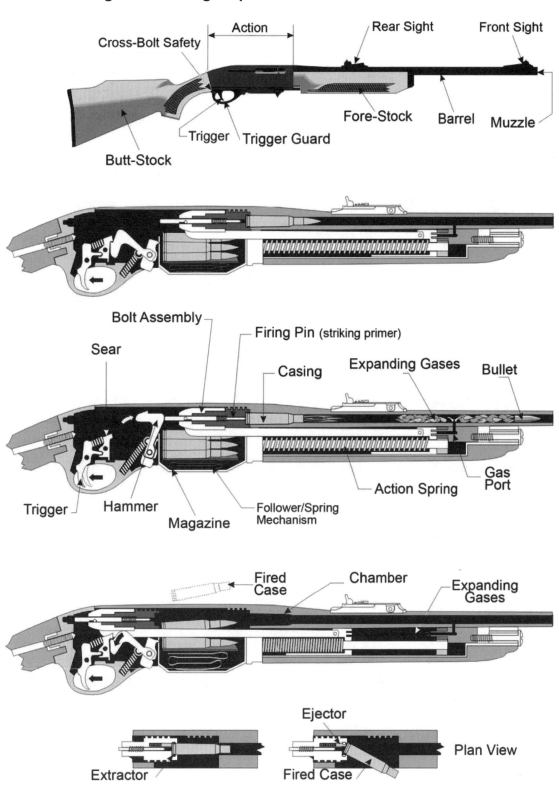

4.13.1 Unloading Procedure - PROVE Safe

 **Before attempting to unload a firearm, follow the Vital Four ACTS.**

1. **P**oint the firearm in the safest available direction throughout the unloading procedure.

    - Make sure that nothing touches the trigger throughout this procedure.

    - Put the safety **ON**, if it can be left on during the unloading process.

2. **R**emove all ammunition as follows:

    - If the magazine (inner tubular or box) is removable, remove the magazine. If applicable, remove any cartridges using gravity to make them fall out (typically from the front of the open end of the tubular magazine).

    - If ammunition cannot be removed in any other way, cycle all the ammunition through the chamber to get them out.

    - Open the action by operating the cocking device (slide or bolt). This should extract and eject any ammunition or empty casing/hull from the chamber.

3. **O**bserve the chamber to confirm that there is no ammunition or empty casing/hull.

4. **V**erify by inspecting the feeding path to make sure it is empty of ammunition, empty casings/hulls, or foreign objects. Make certain you see or feel the follower if one is present.

5. **E**xamine the bore every time you pick up a firearm for lubricant, rust, or obstructions.

The firearm is now unloaded and safe until it leaves the direct control of the person who unloaded and PROVEd it safe.

4.13.2 Loading Procedure

⚠️ **Only load a firearm when you intend to use it, and only in an area where it can be safely and legally discharged.**

1. Prepare the firearm for loading by going through the complete unloading procedure - **PROVE it safe**.

2. Clear any obstructions from the chamber and bore. Clean if required.

3. Where possible, ensure the action is open.

4. Point the firearm in the safest available direction throughout the loading and chambering procedure.

5. Make sure that nothing touches the trigger throughout this process.

6. Put the safety **ON**, if it can be left on during the loading process.

7. Select the correct ammunition by matching the data stamp on the firearm with the head stamp on the cartridge/shell or ammunition box and insert into the magazine.

8. Replace the magazine.

9. Close the action by operating the action release, locking ammunition into the chamber.

10. Put the safety **ON,** if it is not already on.

The firearm is now loaded and ready for use. It requires continuous care and attention until it is unloaded.

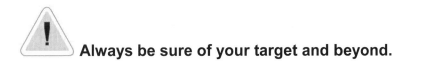 **Always be sure of your target and beyond.**

4.14 Revolver: Single Action, Non-Swing-Out Cylinder (Loading Gate)

4.14.0 Overview

Note: *The following information concerning handguns (see section 4.14 to 4.16) is for information purposes only. Safe use, handling and loading procedures are covered in the Canadian Restricted Firearms Safety Course.*

a. The revolving action takes its name from a revolving cylinder containing a number of cartridge chambers. One chamber at a time lines up with the barrel and hammer (see Figure 46). Revolver cylinders may rotate either clockwise or counter-clockwise, depending on the manufacturer.

b. This action is most commonly found in revolvers that fire single action only. Single action means that the hammer must first be hand cocked before the firearm can be fired by pulling the trigger, (i.e., a single action of the trigger fires the firearm).

c. For the **safety mechanism**, modern revolvers usually have internal safeties designed to prevent them from firing, except when there is a deliberate pull of the trigger.

Figure 46. Single action revolver

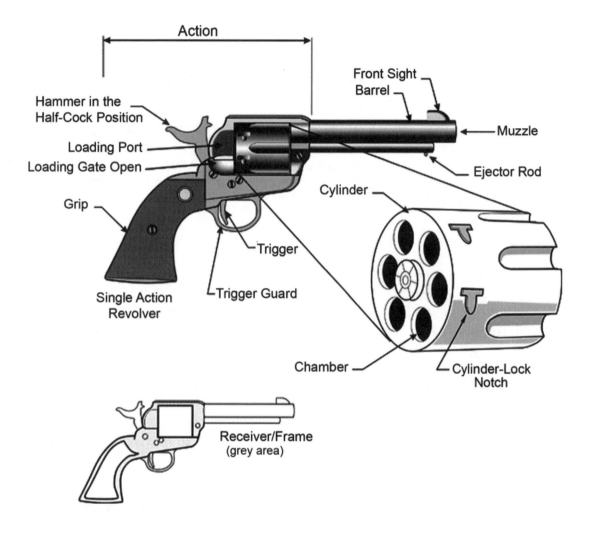

4.14.1 Unloading Procedure - PROVE Safe

Before attempting to unload a firearm, follow the Vital Four ACTS.

1. **P**oint the firearm in the safest available direction throughout the unloading procedure.

   - Make sure that nothing touches the trigger throughout this procedure.

   - Open the loading gate and check if the cylinder will rotate. If the cylinder does NOT rotate, put the safety **ON,** hammer in half-cock/loading notch during the unloading procedure.

2. **R**emove all ammunition as follows:

   - Once the cylinder rotates, observe each chamber through the loading port, as you turn the cylinder, to ensure that there is no ammunition in the cylinder. If any ammunition or casings are present, use the ejector rod under the barrel to remove them. The chamber must be aligned with the loading port.

   - Push the ejector rod from the muzzle to the breech. Let any ammunition or casing fall on the shooting bench or range floor and leave it there until you have completed all steps.

3. **O**bserve every chamber to confirm that there is no ammunition or empty casing(s).

4. **V**erify by inspecting the feeding path to ensure it is clear of ammunition, casings or foreign objects.

5. **E**xamine the bore every time you pick up a firearm for lubricant, rust, or obstructions.

The firearm is now unloaded and safe until it leaves the direct control of the person who unloaded and PROVEd it safe.

4.15 Revolver: Double Action, Swing-Out Cylinder and Break Open

4.15.0 Overview

a. Most swing-out cylinders are double actions. In common usage, the terms are interchangeable. A double action revolver is both cocked and fired by pulling the trigger. Therefore, the trigger performs two actions during one pull.

⚠ **Usually, single action and double action revolvers function equally as single action revolvers.**

b. In addition to the internal mechanisms designed to prevent revolving actions from firing accidentally, swing-out cylinder revolvers also rely on strong double action trigger pull (approximately 6 kg or 13 lbs pressure, compared to a single action trigger pull of approximately 1.5 kg or 3 lbs) as a further safety barrier to accidental firing.

Figure 47. Double action revolver unloading

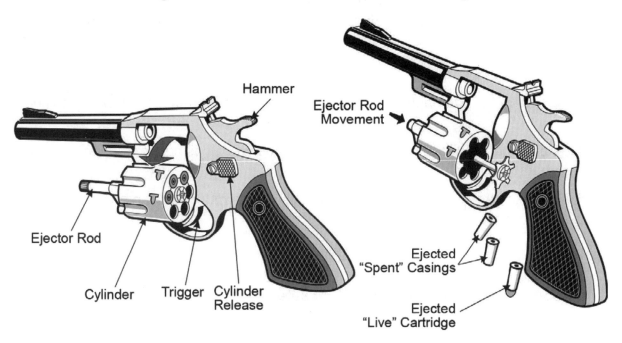

4.15.1 Unloading Procedure - PROVE Safe

 **Before attempting to unload a firearm, follow the Vital Four ACTS.**

1. **P**oint the firearm in the safest available direction throughout the unloading procedure.

   - Make sure that nothing touches the trigger throughout this procedure.

   - Put the safety **ON,** if applicable. While most revolvers do not have safeties, some do. Check your owner's manual or ask a qualified gunsmith.

2. **R**emove all ammunition as follows:

   - Operate the cylinder release and expose the chambers by swinging the cylinder to the side or top.

   - Tip the muzzle slightly upward in a safe direction and operate the ejector rod to allow the ammunition or empty casings to fall out. If not ejected, remove them by hand. Let any ammunition or casing fall on the shooting bench or range floor and leave it there until you have completed all the steps.

   - Leave the action open.

3. **O**bserve the chambers to confirm that there is no ammunition or empty casings.

4. **V**erify that the feeding path is clear of ammunition, casings, or foreign objects.

5. **E**xamine the bore every time you pick up a firearm for lubricant, rust, or obstructions.

The firearm is now unloaded and safe until it leaves the direct control of the person who unloaded and PROVEd it safe.

4.16 Semi-Automatic Actions: Handguns

4.16.0 Overview

a. See Figures 48 & 49. With each pull of the trigger, the semi-automatic action uses part of the energy of the expanding gas from the burning powder to extract the empty cartridge case and to chamber the next cartridge. No hand movement is needed to load another cartridge into the firing position. Each time a cartridge is fired, another cartridge is placed into the chamber from the magazine.

b. Semi-automatic handguns are further divided into single action, double action and double action only. In single action and double action, the hammer stays cocked after each shot is fired. In double action only, the hammer returns to the forward position after each shot is fired.

c. Semi-automatic safeties vary considerably. Most are located near the hammer. If unsure, consult with a qualified gunsmith or the owner's manual.

Figure 48. Single action semi-automatic handgun

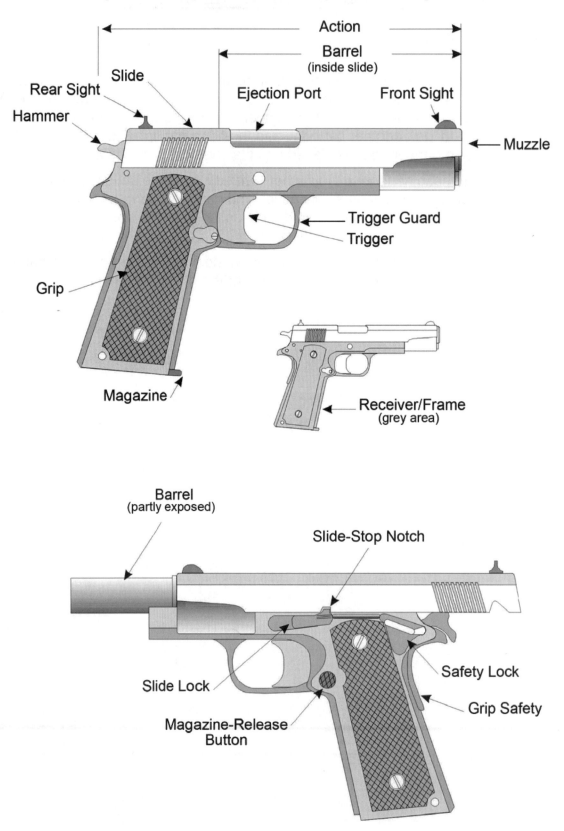

Figure 49. Double action semi-automatic handgun

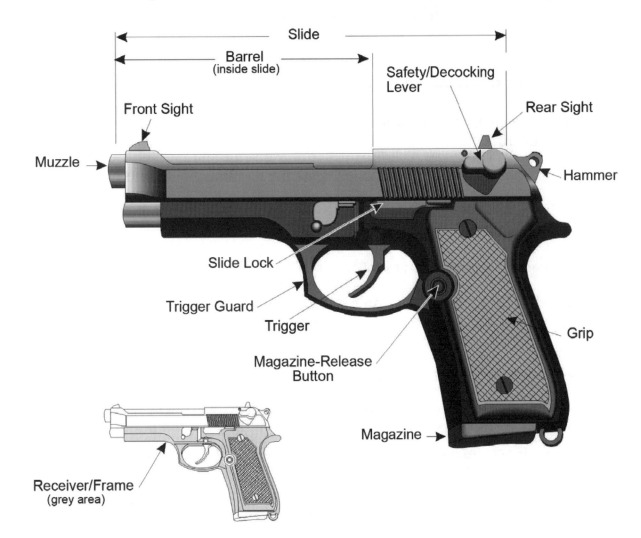

4.16.1 Single Action, Double Action, Double Action Only: Semi-Automatic (Unloading Procedure - PROVE Safe)

Before attempting to unload a firearm, follow the Vital Four ACTS.

1. **P**oint the firearm in the safest available direction throughout the unloading procedure.

   - Make sure that nothing touches the trigger throughout this procedure.

   - Put the safety **ON,** if applicable, if it can be left on during the unloading process.

2. **R**emove all ammunition as follows:

   - Push the magazine release button (see Figure 50) to remove the magazine (the source of all the ammunition except for possibly one chambered cartridge).

   - Pull the slide to the rear by doing the following:

     - Hold the handgun in the strong hand and point in a safe direction. Extend arm, locking wrist and elbow;

     - Pinch the rear of the slide with the weak hand. Ensure your hand does not cover the ejection port;

     - Pull the slide quickly and completely to the rear. This will extract and eject any ammunition or casing from the chamber.

     - Let any ammunition or casing fall on the shooting bench or range floor and leave it there until you have completed all the steps.

   - Locking the slide to the rear, normally by inserting the slide lock into the slide stop notch, where possible (see Figure 51).

3. **O**bserve the chamber to confirm that there is no ammunition or empty casing.

4. **V**erify that the feeding path is clear of ammunition, casings, or foreign objects.

   - **Make certain the magazine has been removed (see Figure 50).**

5. **E**xamine the bore every time you pick up a firearm for lubricant, rust, or obstructions.

The firearm is now unloaded and safe until it leaves the direct control of the person who unloaded and PROVEd it safe.

Figure 50. Removing the magazine from a semi-automatic handgun

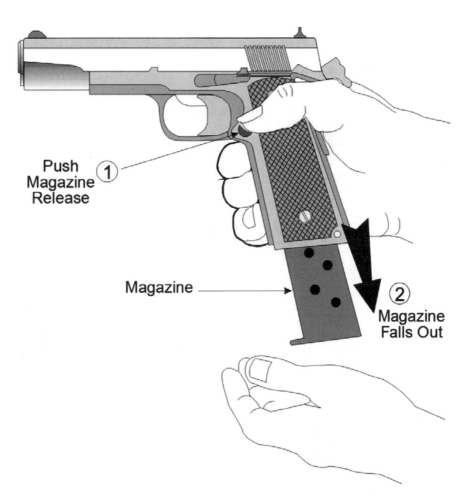

a. Magazine releases are located in different places depending on make and model and may be found in any of the following locations:

- On the grip behind the trigger (see Figure 50)

- At the bottom of the grip (front or rear)

- At some other location

See the owner's manual.

Figure 51. Locking the slide to the rear

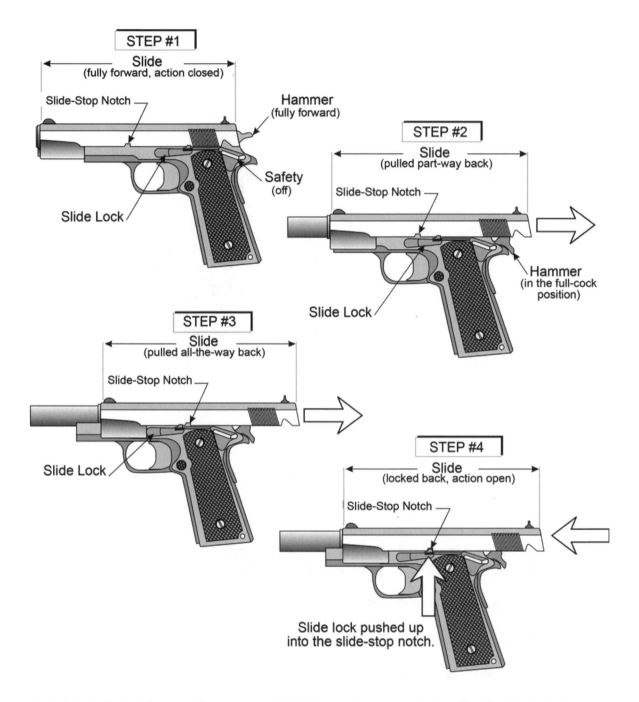

4.16.2 Jammed Cartridges

a. Generally, using commercially made ammunition and a properly maintained firearm, malfunctions will not occur. Firearms jammed with a cartridge or shell in the chamber(s) can be a hazard. This hazard, if not dealt with properly, may result in a serious accident. Consult a qualified person or gunsmith for information on how to perform this function in the safest possible manner with your particular firearm.

4.17 Review Questions

1. Why is it not acceptable to pour black powder directly from a powder container into the muzzle of a muzzleloader?

2. Does the presence of a half-cock notch on a firearm provide an additional safety? Why or why not?

3. State each of the Vital Four ACTS in order.

4. What does PROVE stand for? When is it used?

5. List six different types of safeties.

NOTES:

Section 5

SAFE HANDLING AND
CARRYING OF
NON-RESTRICTED FIREARMS

5 - SAFE HANDLING AND CARRYING OF NON-RESTRICTED FIREARMS

5.0 Overview

a. This section looks at personal safety protection and shows you how to safely handle non-restricted firearms in the following situations:

- Entering or leaving vehicles

- Shooting at a firing range

- Outdoors

- Shooting or hunting with a group

⚠ **Only load a firearm when you intend to use it, and, only in an area where it can be safely and legally discharged. A safe practice is not to chamber a cartridge until ready to fire.**

5.1 Personal Safety Protection

5.1.0 Overview

a. Like many active sports, shooting has the potential to cause personal injury. The careful shooter takes steps to avoid these injuries by wearing personal safety protection.

5.1.1 Eye Protection

a. There is a risk of eye injury in shooting. Shooters going through thick brush can be injured by twigs and branches. Target shooters also risk eye injury. This can come from ejected cartridge casings. It can also come from cartridge casing fragments and other debris ejected during firing.

b. To avoid these hazards, shooters should wear safety glasses made of impact resistant glass or polycarbonate plastic with side shields. They also guard against firearm malfunctions, stray shotgun pellets or bullet fragments.

5.1.2 Hearing Protection

a. Continued unprotected exposure to shooting noise will cause hearing loss. The noise level of a gunshot is similar to that of a jet engine taking off at close range. The need for hearing protection is obvious.

b. Several types of hearing protection are available. On the firing range, shooters should always wear headphone type hearing protectors. These protectors provide reasonable sound protection. They can also be used for years with minimum maintenance.

c. Earplugs are available in several types. Disposable earplugs are made of foam or wax, but they can only be used once.

d. There are also reusable earplugs made of rubber available in several sizes. They require care and cleaning after use.

e. For maximum hearing protection, it is highly recommended that both earplugs and headphone type hearing protectors be worn.

5.1.3 Slips and Falls

a. The risk of slips and falls may occur when handling firearms. This can best be avoided by using common sense.

b. If you do fall, remember your first action should be to control the muzzle of the firearm. This will prevent injury from an accidental discharge. The damage from a fall is probably less than the possible damage from an accidental shot.

c. In the field, pick out the safest trail. Do not depend on surrounding branches to support your weight. Do not cross streams on wet logs or wobbly stones with a loaded firearm.

d. Wearing deep tread high boots will reduce the possibility of slips. They will also protect your ankles and legs from cuts and scrapes.

e. It is recommended that you wear blaze orange when hunting. Some provinces require this by law.

f. Beware of cumbersome clothing like bulky jackets or wading boots. They can cause you to get tangled. They can also interfere with the safe handling of your firearm.

Occasionally, a hot, ejected cartridge casing may come in contact with unprotected skin. This can cause a shooter to flinch. The sudden movement could result in unsafe muzzle control or accidental discharge. Therefore, button up the collar and sleeves of your shirt or blouse. This way, a hot cartridge casing cannot get inside.

5.2 Safe Handling of Firearms in Vehicles

a. The word **vehicle** may include boats, cars, recreational vehicles, snowmobiles, sleds, private aircraft, all terrain vehicles, etc., depending on your particular jurisdiction.

b. Check with provincial or territorial authorities in your area. They can inform you of how the transportation of firearms is regulated locally.

c. When handling firearms around any type of vehicle, follow the steps below:

- **Never have a loaded firearm in or on any vehicle unless you are allowed to shoot from that vehicle**. Unload before entry. Load only after leaving.

- It is especially difficult to control muzzle direction when entering or leaving vehicles. Take extra care to point the muzzle in the safest available direction at such times.

- When a firearm is in a vehicle, it must be placed in a secure position where it will not be dislodged or stepped upon.

Example of an Accident

A duck hunter placed his loaded shotgun into his boat and climbed in. His dog then jumped into the boat, landing on the shotgun. The firearm fired, fatally shooting the hunter in the stomach.

The contributing factors were as follows:
- Unsafe muzzle direction
- Loaded firearm in a vehicle
- Firearm in an unsecured position

5.3 Safety Procedures at the Range

a. Every range has rules of safe behavior. These may vary but will normally include the standard ones shown below:

   1. The muzzle must always be pointed down range.

   2. The action of any firearm must be open at all times except when actually shooting.

   3. Firearms must only be loaded and discharged at the firing line.

   4. No firearm is loaded until the command to load is given by the range officer.

   5. Fingers must be kept out of the trigger guard and off the trigger until the firearm is pointed down range.

   6. Upon the command "cease fire," all firing stops at once. Firearms are unloaded. Actions are opened. Firearms are laid on the mat or on the table. Their muzzles point in a safe direction down range. The shooter steps back from the firing line, behind the cease-fire line.

   7. The Range Officer will inspect each firearm before allowing anyone to go forward of the firing line.

   8. During a cease-fire, no one will handle firearms or ammunition or return to the firing line. At this point, wait for further range commands before any further activity. Persons not engaged in changing targets down range should stand well behind the cease-fire line (see Figure 52).

   9. Use hearing and eye protection.

5.3.1 Additional Range Safety Suggestions

In an emergency, anyone can call a cease-fire.

a. In addition to the above rules, several others we recommend you follow are listed below:

1. Minors and guests should be under direct supervision while shooting.

2. When dealing with minors, all ammunition should be under the control of the immediate supervisor or the range officer. Check with your range for any further restrictions.

3. Firearms should be checked by the range officer on the cease-fire. This is to be sure that all actions are opened and no cartridges are in the breech.

4. Unloaded firearms not in use are to be placed in the rack with the action open or kept in a case. They should be moved with the muzzle pointed in the safest available direction or cased at the firing line.

5. Never allow horseplay, careless handling of firearms or any other distraction while shooting is in progress.

6. Make sure you are using the correct ammunition for your firearm, and as approved by the range.

7. Never shoot at target holders or other range equipment.

8. Do not discharge firearms outside of designated range property or posted range use times.

Figure 52. Range layout

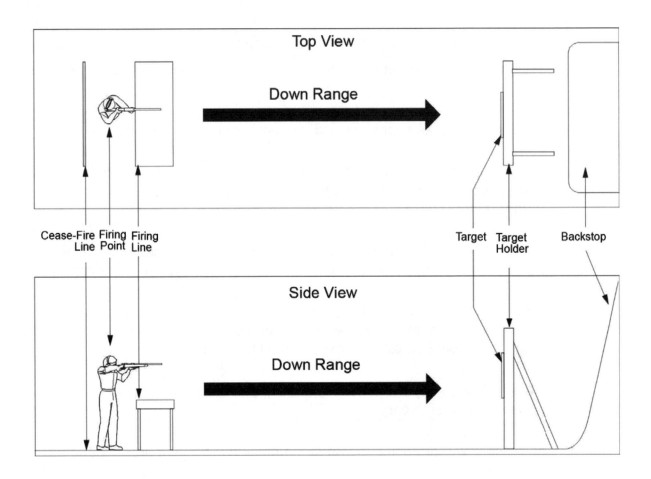

5.4 Range Courtesy

a. There are certain standards of range courtesy. Considerate shooters follow them. Some of these standards are listed below:

1. Rules and procedures very between ranges. Check and obey local rules. There should be a safety briefing before starting.

2. Sign in to the firing range upon arrival, if required.

3. Avoid interrupting or distracting others when they are shooting.

4. Do not smoke on the firing line.

5. Ask the owner's or shooter's permission before handling that person's firearm or equipment.

6. Leave enough space between you and others to ensure safety.

7. If firing particularly smokey firearms, shoot from downwind of other shooters on the firing line. Black powder firearms are especially smokey.

8. Do not fire on other people's targets, targets not directly down range from yourself or any target that may disturb others.

9. Those firing semi-automatic firearms should take a firing point where other people will not be disturbed by ejected casings.

10. Rapid firing may disturb shooters sighting-in or doing deliberate target work.

11. Clean up after shooting. Pick up cartridge casings. Take down targets.

12. Put away any range-owned equipment you have used. For example, sandbags or bench rests.

5.5 Range Commands

a. The following are examples of typical range commands:

- "The range is active."

- "Cease-fire."

- "The range is no longer active."

⚠ **Range commands and signals vary between shooting sports, ranges and jurisdictions. Be sure you are aware of and clearly understand the commands used in your area. If you are unsure, ask the Range Officer or a local official before you go to the range (see Appendix I: Visual Range Signals and Devices).**

5.6 Safe Handling of Firearms Outdoors

a. Always remember that people or livestock you cannot see may be close enough to be injured. Be aware of the **dangerous range** of your firearm and ammunition.

b. **Control the muzzle direction at all times**. Keep the safety "ON" until you are ready to use the firearm.

c. Under all circumstances, protect the trigger and safety while carrying your firearm. A twig or branch may catch the trigger, put the safety off, or swing the muzzle around.

d. When carrying a firearm, remember that you can slip and fall, causing an accidental discharge. Plan how to protect the firearm and control its direction when you fall, and, if possible, unload it before crossing uneven ground or ice.

e. **Always be sure of your target and beyond**. Don't shoot at game near the top of a hill. People or livestock may be in the line of fire over the hill. Never shoot near a building without permission. Someone may be using it as a shelter.

f. Water, rocks or flat surfaces may cause the bullet to break up or ricochet. Use caution.

g. When you cross a fence or other obstacle, unload your firearm and **leave the action open**. The same goes for areas that are slippery, rocky or uneven.

h. When crossing a fence alone, unload the firearm and place the firearm under the fence. Make sure the firearm is flat on the ground with the action open and the muzzle pointed away from where you are crossing (see Figure 53).

i. If you are in a group, one person should stand away from the crossing point. This person should hold the unloaded and open firearms while the others cross the obstacle (see Figure 54).

j. When hunting alone from a pit, unload your firearm and place it outside before entering. Then enter and bring the unloaded firearm into the pit after you.

k. **Remember to check your firearm for dirt if you lay it on the ground. This is especially important for the muzzle.**

Use binoculars if you need to see something more clearly. Never use a scope mounted on a firearm as a substitute for binoculars to identify persons, animals or objects.

Figure 53. Individual crossing a fence safely

Figure 54. Group crossing a fence safely

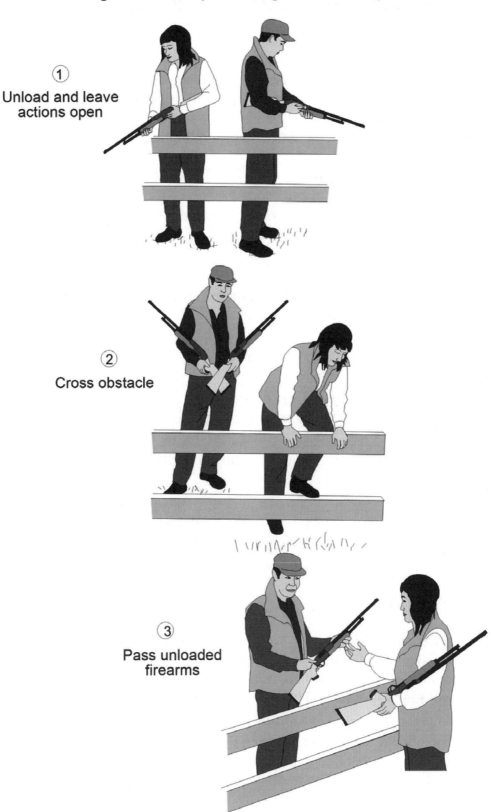

5.7 Shooting or Hunting with a Group

5.7.0 Overview

a. Any shot fired in the wrong direction might hit another person in your group. Make sure safe zones of fire are established to prevent such incidents. It is very important to follow the safety rules in this handbook. The rules in section 5.7.1 are especially important for shooting or hunting with a group.

5.7.1 Informal Firing Line

a. An informal firing line is a very effective method to use when sighting-in or target shooting with a group of two or more people. Follow these basic safety steps below:

1. Appoint someone as the range officer. This person will be responsible for supervising all of the following steps.

2. Follow the normal range commands and procedures.

3. Set up a firing line. Firearms may only be uncased, handled and loaded at this firing line. This must be done under the range officer's direction.

4. Be sure that the appointed range officer explains the procedures to everyone in the group.

5. Decide on which direction is down-range. Make sure there is a safe backstop. This will be the only direction in which muzzles can be pointed and firearms fired.

5.7.2 Safe Zones of Fire

a. It is worth emphasizing again. Any shot fired in the wrong direction by a group member might hit another person. This is true for all shooting situations. To prevent this, before starting, everybody should agree on which area each shooter will cover (see Figure 55). This will clearly define each individual's safe zone of fire.

b. Positions change when you advance through the field. You should always know exactly where your shooting partners are. Guard both them and yourself against being accidentally shot.

Figure 55. Safe zones of fire

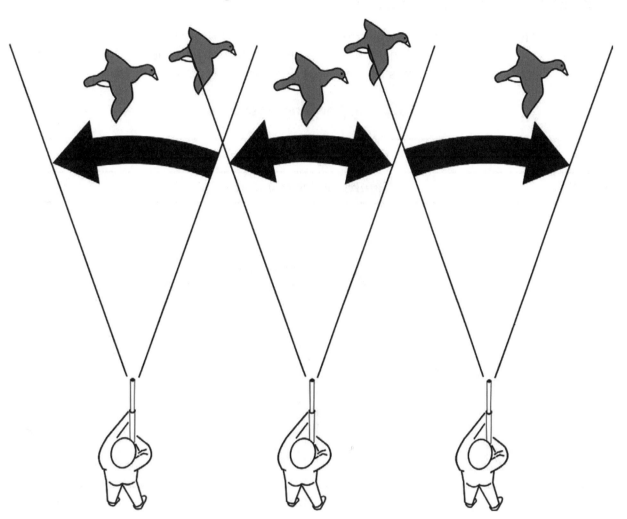

 Always know exactly where your shooting partners, or others, are.

5.8 Carrying Positions

a. **Muzzle direction is all-important when carrying firearms.** You can control muzzle direction safely only if you use proper carrying positions. When carrying firearms, you must always be aware of the possibility of slips or falls.

Table 10. Carrying Positions

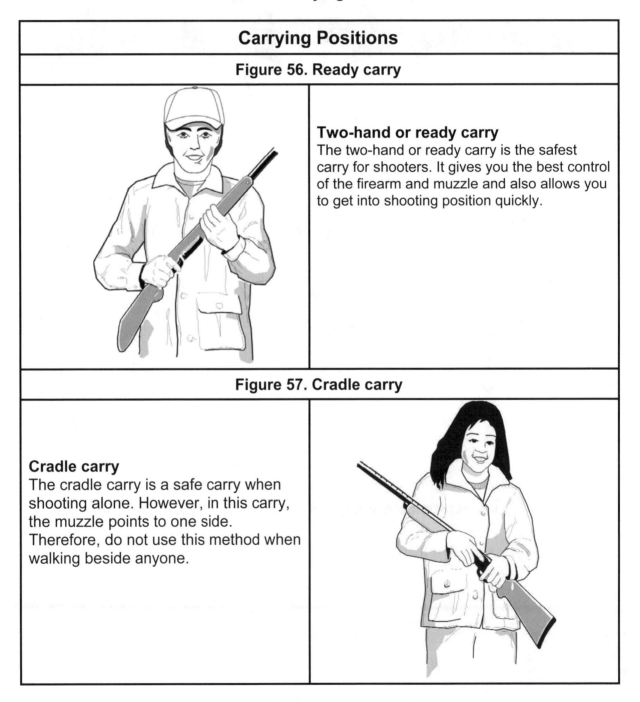

Carrying Positions
Figure 56. Ready carry

Two-hand or ready carry
The two-hand or ready carry is the safest carry for shooters. It gives you the best control of the firearm and muzzle and also allows you to get into shooting position quickly.

Figure 57. Cradle carry

Cradle carry
The cradle carry is a safe carry when shooting alone. However, in this carry, the muzzle points to one side. Therefore, do not use this method when walking beside anyone.

Figure 58. Elbow or side carry (action open)

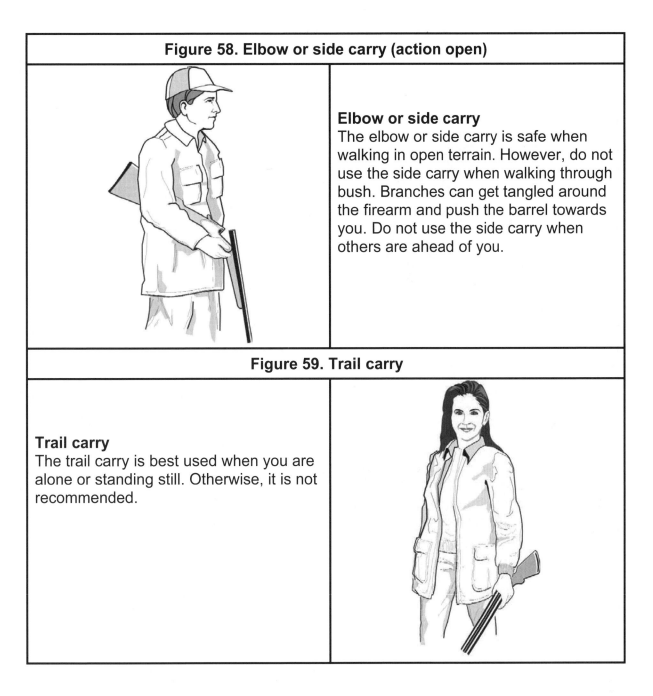

Elbow or side carry
The elbow or side carry is safe when walking in open terrain. However, do not use the side carry when walking through bush. Branches can get tangled around the firearm and push the barrel towards you. Do not use the side carry when others are ahead of you.

Figure 59. Trail carry

Trail carry
The trail carry is best used when you are alone or standing still. Otherwise, it is not recommended.

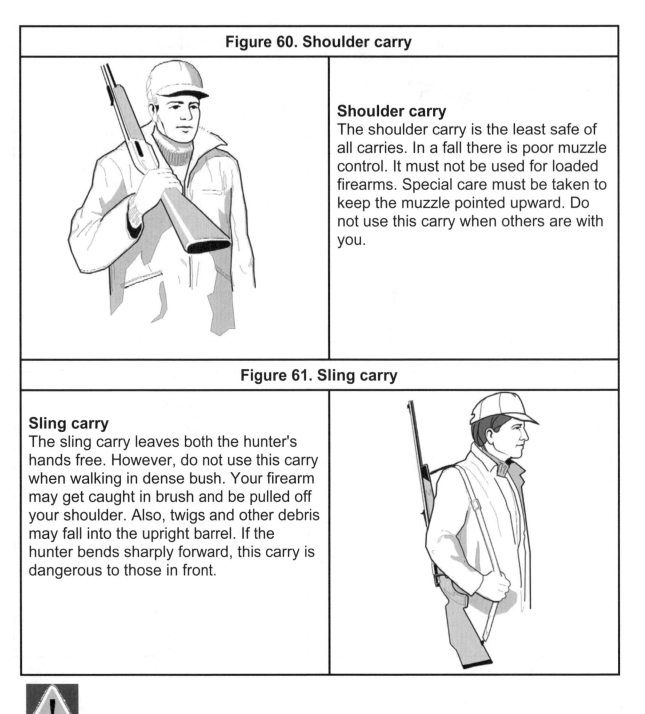

Figure 60. Shoulder carry

Shoulder carry
The shoulder carry is the least safe of all carries. In a fall there is poor muzzle control. It must not be used for loaded firearms. Special care must be taken to keep the muzzle pointed upward. Do not use this carry when others are with you.

Figure 61. Sling carry

Sling carry
The sling carry leaves both the hunter's hands free. However, do not use this carry when walking in dense bush. Your firearm may get caught in brush and be pulled off your shoulder. Also, twigs and other debris may fall into the upright barrel. If the hunter bends sharply forward, this carry is dangerous to those in front.

Which carry you use will depend on where your companions are and the kind of terrain you are in. Never use a carry that will cause the muzzle to be pointed at another person.

5.9 Review Questions

1. Can the scope mounted on your firearm be used as a substitute for binoculars to identify persons, animals or objects?

2. Describe the procedure for crossing an obstacle safely.

3. State what action must be taken when a cease-fire is called.

4. Name the six different firearm carry positions. Which one is the safest? Which one is the least safe? Why?

NOTES:

Section 6

FIRING TECHNIQUES AND PROCEDURES FOR NON-RESTRICTED FIREARMS

6 – FIRING TECHNIQUES AND PROCEDURES FOR NON-RESTRICTED FIREARMS

6.0 Introduction to Marksmanship

a. Marksmanship is the ability to hit your mark or target. Good marksmanship is important for safe shooting. If you are not certain where the bullet will go, how can the shot be safe?

b. Marksmanship depends on many factors, including anticipation, shooting position, aim, trigger control, controlled breathing and follow-through. These factors are discussed in this section.

6.1 Anticipation

a. When using a firearm, you must always be thinking about the possible situations and shots that may occur. The following are some examples:

1. Will game appear suddenly?

2. Where are the others in my shooting group?

3. Is there a chance the bullet will be deflected by a tree, a rock or water?

4. Could someone be just over that hill?

5. Where will the bullet go if it passes completely through the target?

 **Always judge the possible results of every shot carefully before firing.**

6.2 Shooting Positions

6.2.0 Overview

⚠️ If you are left-handed, reverse the procedures for each shooting position. Left-handed shooters should consider using firearms manufactured specifically for left-handed use.

6.2.1 Rifles

a. The four shooting positions for rifles are as follows:

1. Standing position

2. Kneeling position

3. Sitting position

4. Prone position

1. Standing Position

i.   The standing position is the least stable shooting position from which to fire (see Figure 62).

ii.   To shoot from the standing position, first, turn your body approximately 45° to the right of the target. Place your feet shoulder width apart. Support the rifle with your left arm and hand. Hold the left arm against your body for extra support where possible. Hold the stock firmly against your shoulder with the right hand. Keep holding the rifle firmly but not tightly.

iii. If there is too much waver, do not shoot. Rest or support the rifle on a stable object such as a tree or large rock. In such situations, padding beneath the firearm is recommended. Using a sling will help steady your shot.

Figure 62. Standing position

2. Kneeling Position

i.   The kneeling position (see Figure 63) is better than the standing position but not as steady as either the prone or sitting positions.

ii. Turn to about a 45° angle to the target. Kneel on your right knee and place your left foot slightly forward. Sit on the heel or the side of the right foot. Place the left elbow near but not on the bony part of the left knee, as far under the rifle as you can.

Figure 63. Kneeling position

3. Sitting Position

i. The sitting position is one of the steadiest shooting positions (see Figure 64).

ii. Sit solidly on the ground, with your legs crossed or open, and your body positioned about 30° to the right of the line of aim.

iii. Place your left elbow near, but not on, the bony part of the left knee. Tuck the elbow as far under the rifle as possible. Place the right elbow on or near the right knee.

iv. Hold the rifle firmly but do not grip it tightly. If bracing your body against a tree or rock to steady your aim, be careful that the recoil will not force you against the support.

Figure 64. Sitting position

4. Prone Position

i.   The prone position is the steadiest shooting position (see Figure 65). It is good for firing accurate long distance shots if tall grass or dense brush does not obscure the line of sight to the target.

ii. If right-handed, lie on your stomach with your body angled slightly to the left of the line of aim. Keep your back straight and legs in a relaxed position. The right leg should be bent slightly. Both elbows should be bent and your shoulders curved slightly forward to form a solid upper body position. The upper body and arms support the rifle weight.

iii. When shooting, you can use a rifle sling for extra support. Hold the rifle grip with the trigger hand. Place your opposite arm through the sling as far as it will go. Swing your arm in an outward circular motion, ending with your hand under the fore-stock of the rifle and the sling across the back of your hand.

Figure 65. Prone position

6.2.2 Shotguns

a. Shooting a shotgun is different from shooting a rifle. With a rifle you aim precisely. With a shotgun you point at the target (see Figure 66). Some shotguns are equipped with adjustable sights and are primarily used to fire slugs.

b. Accurate shotgun shooting requires you to make a fast but smooth series of movements of the eyes, body and firearm. To achieve this, stand like a boxer: feet spread apart, well-balanced, arms and body free to swing right or left. This position allows rapid movement.

c. When firing, shift your body weight to the leading leg (left leg if you shoot right-handed, and vice versa). The leading hand holds the shotgun fore-end and points naturally to the target area. Aim the shotgun by pointing it at the target and tapping the trigger instead of squeezing it. With moving targets, continue to follow through as you fire. Otherwise, the shot will miss behind the target.

Figure 66. Shotgun shooting position

6.3 Aiming Your Firearm

6.3.0 Overview

a. Most sights are mounted on the top of the barrel. Their purpose is to help the shooter aim accurately (see Figure 67).

b. There are four main types of sights:

    1. Open sights

    2. Peep sights (also called aperture sights)

    3. Telescopic sights (also called optical sights)

    4. Electronic sights

c. Rifles and handguns may have any of these types.

d. Most shotguns have only a bead mounted on the front of the barrel. This serves as a front sight.

Figure 67. Types of sights

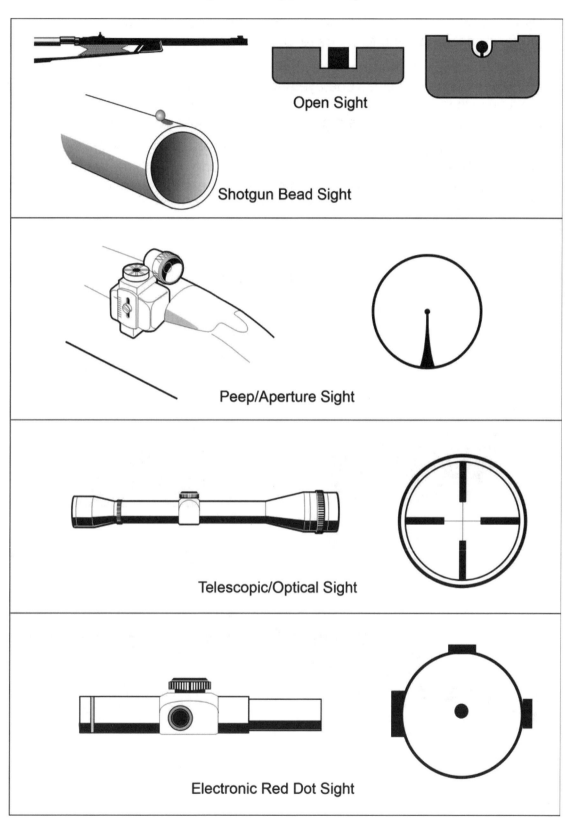

Open Sight

Shotgun Bead Sight

Peep/Aperture Sight

Telescopic/Optical Sight

Electronic Red Dot Sight

6.3.1 Aiming Rifles

a. Use your master eye for sighting. It is the stronger of your two eyes and will judge speed, range and focus more accurately.

b. To find out which is your master eye, point your finger at a distant object with both eyes open. First close one eye and then the other. Your finger will remain lined up with the object when your master eye is open. Always try to aim with both eyes open as this gives a better view of the area surrounding the target.

c. You must also learn to correctly use your firearm's sight if your aim is to be accurate. Open sights require you to physically line up both rear and front sights with the target. This process is called **sight alignment.** When you aim any sight at a target, a **sight picture** is created (see Figure 68).

Figure 68. Open sights aligned on a target

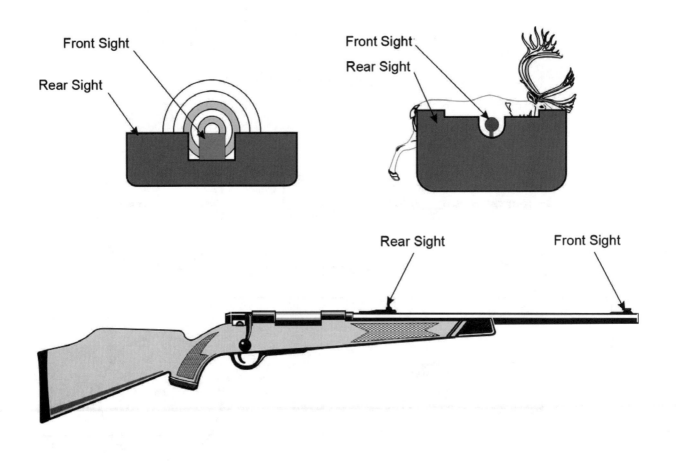

d. Scope and electronic red dot sights do not require conscious alignment. Scope sights also have the advantage of magnifying your view of the target (see fig. 69).

e. When preparing to aim through a scope or electronic red dot sight, do not look away from the target and then try to find the target again by looking through the scope. Instead, while steadily watching the target, mount the firearm correctly to your shoulder pointing the firearm toward the target area until the scope comes up naturally between your eye and the target. Keep your eye well clear of the sight when firing.

⚠ **Scope sights have a very narrow field of view, so you might not see a person or object coming into the path of your shot. Never use a mounted scope as a substitute for binoculars to identify persons, animals or objects.**

Figure 69. Aperture and scope sights aligned on a target

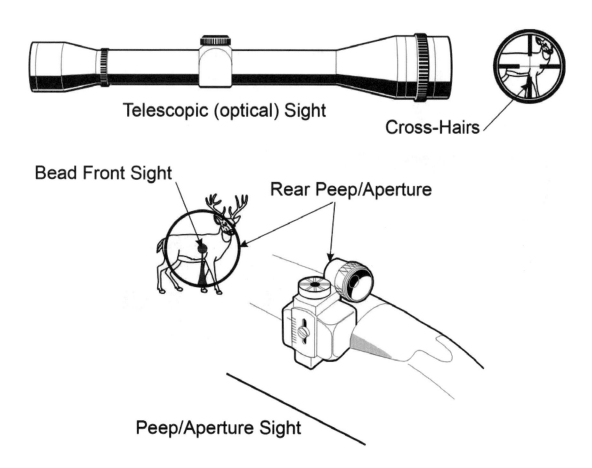

Telescopic (optical) Sight

Cross-Hairs

Bead Front Sight

Rear Peep/Aperture

Peep/Aperture Sight

6.3.2 Pointing Shotguns

a. Pointing a shotgun is different from aiming other firearms. With a rifle, you must aim precisely. With a shotgun, you point at the target. When a shotgun is fired, the shot pellets spread out after leaving the barrel and hit a larger area than a single bullet. Therefore, precise aiming is not as necessary as with a rifle.

b. When using a shotgun, keep both eyes open. Focus on the moving target, not on the firearm barrel or the bead sight. While watching the target, place the shotgun to your shoulder and point it toward the target area. Be sure to place the stock against your cheek first, then against your shoulder. This positions the firearm in exactly the same position each time you shoot (see Figure 70).

c. Some shotguns are equipped with adjustable sights and are primarily used to fire slugs. For this type of shotgun, use the same aiming techniques as you would for a rifle.

Figure 70. Shotgun sight alignment

Close Up of Clay Target

6.4 Trigger Control

a. Trigger control is essential for accurate shooting.

1. Rifles

When the sights are aligned on the target, squeeze the trigger slowly and steadily. Avoid yanking or pulling. Anything other than a smooth squeeze will cause the firearm to waver and send the shot off target. Relax before the firearm fires to allow each shot to happen almost as a "surprise".

2. Shotguns

Shotgun triggers are tapped instead of squeezed. The trigger tap is similar to the action of striking a typewriter key. Tap the trigger quickly, but not hard.

6.5 Controlled Breathing

a. You need to control your breathing to shoot accurately. The firearm barrel will move unless you control your breathing when you fire.

b. When you are in shooting position, take a few deep breaths. Exhale a portion of the last one. Hold your breath while you aim and squeeze the trigger. This will help you keep the sights on the target.

c. If you hold your breath too long (more than about 8 seconds), you may lose your concentration and miss the target. If you run out of breath before firing, take another breath and re-aim.

6.6 Follow-Through

a. Follow-through simply means maintaining your sight picture and/or shooting position, after discharging the firearm. If you do not follow through, it is more likely that your shot will be off target.

6.7 Targets

a. Acceptable Targets

Before firing at any target, verify the target by asking yourself the questions below:

- Am I sure of the identity of my target?

- Can I see it clearly?

- Am I positive it is exactly the target I want?

- Is it a permitted target?

- Is it legal game?

- Is it the proper target at a shooting range?

- Is anything else in the line of fire, either in front or beside or behind the target?

- Is it on a hilltop or across a road?

- Could anything else come suddenly into the line of fire?

b. Unacceptable Targets

The following are unacceptable targets:

- Any target which, when fired upon, may damage or litter private or public property (this includes signs, wire insulators, bottles, old buildings, parked equipment and abandoned cars);

- Illegal game (this includes out of season, non game or endangered species);

- Any target which, when fired upon, might endanger the safety of others; special attention is required when shooting near inhabited areas, across or along roads, over hills, and at water or hard surfaces;

- Any target which, when fired upon, may disturb others, for example, discharging firearms early in the morning or near dwellings;

- Any target or a material or shape that can cause ricochets;

- Any target made of glass or other material that causes fragment hazards.

6.8 Review Questions

1. Why should you follow through when shooting a moving target?

2. Describe the four shooting positions for rifles. Which of the four provides the steadiest aim?

3. State at least three questions you should ask yourself before firing at any target.

4. Provide at least three examples of unacceptable targets.

NOTES:

Section 7

CARE OF
NON-RESTRICTED
FIREARMS

7 – CARE OF NON-RESTRICTED FIREARMS

7.1 Firearm Servicing

⚠ **Ensure that all firearms are unloaded and PROVEd safe before attempting to clean. Refer to Section 4 on unloading procedures - PROVE.**

a. Always be sure your firearm is functioning properly. A firearm that does not work properly is an unsafe firearm.

b. This section on minor maintenance and servicing procedures for your firearm is included for general information only. Specific information on cleaning and servicing your firearm is available in your firearm owner's manual, at a gun shop, or from a gunsmith. Accidents can occur if these procedures are not performed correctly.

c. Firearms are precision instruments. Even minor repairs should be made by qualified individuals. **Unqualified persons should never try to repair or modify any firearm.**

d. **The average user should do basic cleaning and lubrication only.**

Example of an accident

Someone was preparing to clean a loaded firearm with the action closed, and dropped it. The rifle fired when it hit the floor. Someone in the next room was killed.

The contributing factors were as follows:
- Having a loaded firearm in a house
- Lack of muzzle control
- Failing to **PROVE** the firearm unloaded
- Action was closed

7.2 Firearm Cleaning

7.2.0 Overview

a. Information on cleaning firearms safely may be obtained from your firearm owner's manual. If you do not have one, contact the manufacturer. Accidents can happen if the cleaning procedure is not performed correctly.

b. The two major threats to firearm safety are the following:

    1. Rust caused by moisture and condensation

    2. Excessive build-up of residue or rust in the firearm

c. Either may cause excessive pressure, damaging the barrel. This is why regular cleaning is recommended.

d. The barrel of a firearm should be cleaned after every use. This will protect its finish. It will also help keep it in good working order. For instructions on cleaning the rest of the firearm, check your owner's manual.

e. Modern smokeless primers and powders are non-corrosive. However, some older military surplus ammunition still contains corrosive chemicals. If you use corrosive ammunition, you should clean your firearm immediately after you use it.

f. Any firearm that has been stored for a long time must be cleaned thoroughly **before** use. **Cleaning before using** is required when the firearm has been exposed to moisture or dirt.

If cleaning your firearm requires disassembly, consult your owner's manual. You should wear safety glasses if disassembly is required. Oil or moisture can be very dangerous in cold weather. They may cause safeties and other firing mechanism parts to freeze in a firing position. Later, when the firearm thaws, it may fire. Residue or rust in the chamber or barrel may cause serious pressure build-up. Also, oil may mix with unburnt powder and other dirt, causing the firearm to jam.

7.2.1 Cleaning Materials

a. To clean a firearm properly, you need the following materials:

- A cleaning rod or a pull-through and attachments (be sure to use the right size for the firearm), such as:

    - A bore brush

    - Tips to hold cloth patches;

- Patches

- Powder solvent (also called "bore cleaner")

- Light gun oil, and

- A soft cloth.

b. If possible, clean your firearm from the breech toward the muzzle. Avoid cleaning from the muzzle toward the breech (see Figures 71 & 72 in section 7.2.2).

c. However, you may have to clean some types from the muzzle end. In this case, lock the breech open. This permits the passage of the cleaning rod completely through the barrel. You will find a pull-through cleaning device helpful. Avoid rubbing the cleaning rod on the muzzle. Damage to the muzzle may occur. It is beneficial to insert a cloth into the open action to collect residue, to prevent dirt from entering the action, and to prevent damage to the firearm.

d. When cleaning a bolt action, remove the bolt, if possible. Clean the firearm from the breech end. Some firearms are easier to clean if you remove the barrel first.

While cleaning a firearm, remember and follow the Vital Four ACTS. The following additional recommended practices for home safety with firearms might prevent accidents:

- **Make sure no ammunition is nearby during cleaning.**

- **Never allow a loaded firearm in any building or living area.**

- **Always give cleaning your firearm your full attention. Never clean a firearm while doing something else, like watching television.**

7.2.2 Cleaning Procedure

a. The firearms cleaning procedures are as follows:

1. Attach the bore brush to the cleaning rod. Apply bore cleaner to the brush.

2. Run the brush through the bore of the firearm barrel several times. Be sure that the brush sticks out from the barrel completely. Then, draw it back through the barrel (see Figure 71).

3. Remove the bore brush from the cleaning rod. Attach a patch-holder tip and a proper size cloth patch. Pour solvent on the cloth patch. Run it through the bore several times. Remove the cloth patch from the rod tip.

4. Next, run a clean, dry patch through the bore several times.

5. If the patch comes out dirty, repeat the first four steps. Do this until a patch finally comes through clean.

6. Next, run a lightly oiled patch through the bore. Use only light gun oil.

7. Wipe the outside of the firearm with a clean cloth and apply a light coat of gun oil or rust preventative to the metal surfaces. You should also maintain the condition of the stock by applying the appropriate treatment (see the owner's manual).

8. Always store your firearm properly.

Figure 71. Cleaning a rifle barrel from the breech to the muzzle

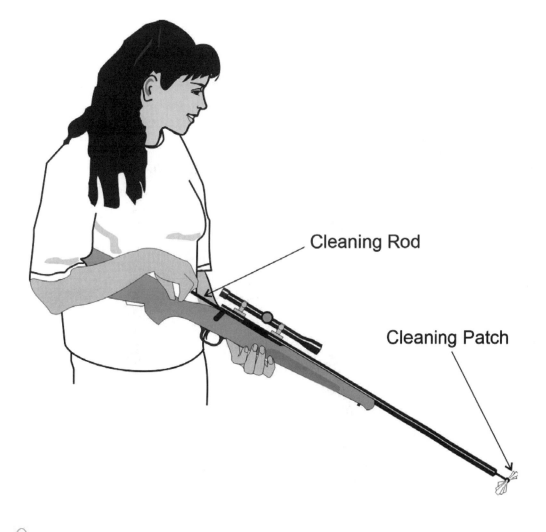

Cleaning Rod

Cleaning Patch

⚠️ After cleaning a firearm for storage, avoid skin contact with metal parts. Acids in perspiration can cause rust.

b. Remember, before the next firing of the firearm, run a dry patch through the barrel to remove any oil.

Figure 72. Cleaning a rifle

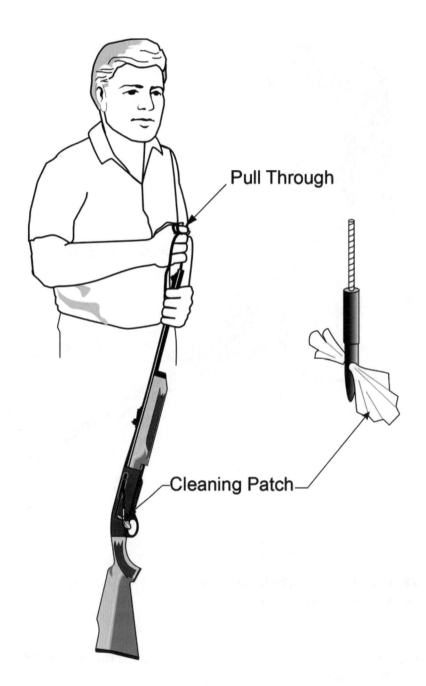

7.2.3 Cleaning a Muzzleloader

a. A black powder firearm must be properly cleaned after every firing session. Black powder is very corrosive. It attracts moisture, which causes rust.

b. Cleaning black powder firearms improperly can result in carbon buildup in the barrel, which may cause **coking.** This condition may cause a glowing ember to remain after firing, resulting in a dangerous situation if the firearm is reloaded.

c. Use either commercial black powder cleaning solvent or hot, soapy water.

d. You will also need a ramrod with a cleaning patch attached. Use a rod as close to the bore diameter as possible. Refer to the owner's manual.

e. Use wet patches to soften the dried powder.

1. Detach the barrel and place the lock end in a container of soapy water.

2. Attach a patch to the ramrod. Insert the ramrod into the barrel. Pump the ramrod up and down until water flows from the top end of the barrel.

3. Repeat step 2. Change the water as it becomes dirty. Repeat until the water stays clean.

4. Dry the barrel out with several dry patches. Oil thoroughly with good gun oil.

5. Remove the lock for cleaning and oiling after every use.

It is strongly recommended that individuals interested in muzzleloading seek additional training from qualified experts in the field.

7.2.4 Cleaning Ammunition

a. Ammunition should also be kept clean and dry. Oil, sand or dirt on the cartridge or shell can damage the firearm. It could also cause jamming of the action.

b. Avoid exposing your ammunition to heat and vibration. Powder can decay and become unpredictable if exposed to excessive heat and long-term vibration.

Primers are adversely affected by exposure to penetrating oils. Do not clean your ammunition with an oily rag. Before using any firearm, remove oil or grease from inside the barrel. Increased pressure caused by dirt or oil may cause the barrel to burst. This comes from the pressure generated in a dirty barrel when a bullet is fired through it. After storage, and before you use the firearm again, run a clean patch through the bore. Remove all grease and oil. Always ensure your firearm is in good working order. Ensure that you have followed the Vital Four ACTS in order to PROVE the firearm safe before attempting to clean and throughout the entire cleaning procedure. Refer to section 4 on unloading procedures.

7.3 Review Questions

1. Explain why a firearm should be cleaned regularly.

2. What is the first step to take when preparing to clean a firearm?

3. Why should oil or grease be removed from inside the barrel of a firearm?

NOTES:

Section 8

SOCIAL RESPONSIBILITIES
OF THE
FIREARMS OWNER/USER

8 - SOCIAL RESPONSIBILITIES OF THE FIREARMS OWNER/USER

8.1 Firearm-Related Deaths and Injuries

a. The main purpose of this course is to promote the safe use and handling of firearms. Increased safety awareness will help prevent both the accidental and deliberate misuse of firearms.

b. Most safety courses concentrate on the prevention of accidents caused by careless use or unintentional discharge of firearms. However, the intentional misuse of firearms in suicides and homicides results in far more deaths and serious injuries.

c. Suicides and homicides are often acts of sudden impulse. Many of them might not have happened if the firearms and ammunition were stored safely. For this reason, this course stresses the safe handling and use of non-restricted firearms and ammunition, and their secure storage.

8.2 Intentional Misuse of Firearms

8.2.0 Overview

a. The intentional misuse of firearms, resulting in suicide and homicide, has fallen since the eighties. Unintentional misuse of firearms, resulting in accidents, has also fallen.

b. The misuse of firearms can lead to tragic results. Firearms are not unique that way. This is also true of automobiles, power tools, and even kitchen knives.

8.2.1 Suicide

a. In Canada, the great majority of firearm-related deaths are suicides.

b. In many cases, suicide is an act of sudden impulse. It is often brought on by some temporary setback or moment of depression. These occurrences may seem trivial to the outside observer. They are not trivial to the person experiencing them. Even a failed exam, an argument with a girlfriend or boyfriend, or an accident with the family car can bring it on.

Examples of Suicide and Attempted Suicide

1. A young man of 18 had an accident with his father's truck. When he got home, the father scolded him. The father then left to examine the truck at the repair shop. The young man got his father's rifle that was kept unsecured at home. He loaded a cartridge into it and shot himself. This was not the first time he had tried suicide. But this time he succeeded.

2. A young man broke up with his girlfriend. He went home where a rifle and ammunition were kept in an unlocked closet. He shot himself in the face. Surgery saved his life but he lost an eye. He says that if no firearm had been readily available, he would not have attempted suicide. That was twenty years ago. He has not tried again.

The contributing factors were as follows:

- Firearm not locked or stored securely
- Ammunition not stored properly

 One line of defense against suicide is delayed access to firearms.

c. Many people think that a person trying to commit suicide will just find another method if a firearm is not available. Studies show that this is not always true. If a weapon cannot be found right away, some individuals contemplating suicide give the idea up and never try again.

d. Even if another method is used, it may not be as lethal as a firearm. Those people who survive a suicide attempt, quite often do not try again. In fact, a few weeks later, many survivors are pleased they were not successful. With a firearm, a suicidal person often does not get a second chance.

8.2.2 Homicide

a. Homicide means the intentional killing of another human being. In Canada, this is the second highest cause of death related to firearms.

b. Like suicides, there are common misunderstandings about homicides. For example, a significant number of homicides are carried out by people with no criminal record.

c. If a firearm is available in these situations, it is more likely to be used. If not a firearm, another weapon may be used in the heat of the moment, like a fist, a club or a knife. But the chances of killing someone with them are lower than with a firearm.

d. Many suicides and homicides are acts of sudden, temporary impulse. The majority of these acts are carried out by people in their own homes while under great strain. Often, alcohol or drug abuse is also involved.

Example of Homicide

1. A husband and wife were in the process of separating. He was unemployed; she was not. Family, friends and neighbours knew they were having violent disputes. The police did not. Shortly after the husband became aware that his wife wanted to confirm their permanent separation, and after he was informed that she was involved with another man, he took a shotgun and killed her. He was under the influence of alcohol. After committing the murder, the husband remained at the scene.

The contributing factors were as follows:
- Easy access to firearms and ammunition
- Alcohol
- No alternate storage of firearms used

---

e. What can the average firearm owner do about this? Impulse and availability of firearms and ammunition are two factors. If there is no easy access, the impulse to act in a violent way often weakens in a few minutes or hours.

Examples of Homicide

2. A husband kept a 12-gauge shotgun under a bed. During a family argument, the husband went and got it. He had been drinking. He wanted to threaten his wife. The firearm discharged and killed her.

3. A man was having a heated argument with some people in a bar. As a result, he was thrown out of the bar. He went home and took his father's rifle from a gun rack. He also took ammunition from a shelf below. He returned to the bar and fired into the crowded room from the doorway. He killed one person and wounded two others.

The contributing factors were as follows:

- Easy access to firearms and ammunition
- Alcohol

 Be sure your firearms and ammunition are properly stored. Make them difficult to get at. Store each away separately and locked securely.

8.2.3 Signs of Risk

a. As noted in the previous examples, sometimes it is possible to detect the signs that someone may be at risk of committing suicide or homicide. You can sometimes anticipate violent situations before they happen. Remember, these events can happen in our own homes or those of friends or neighbours.

b. When these situations seem to be developing, it is good practice to remove all firearms. This is true even if they are properly stored. Consider storing the firearms at an alternate location, and, if necessary, notify the police of the situation.

Example of Storing Firearms at an Alternate Location

A ten-year old boy died suddenly of an accident at home. The parents were very upset, and the police who were at the scene asked if firearms were present in the household. When the father said that he owned two rifles and a shotgun, the police requested permission to take the firearms and store them at the police station for a few days. The father agreed. He picked up his firearms one week later, and he agreed with police that persons who face such a tragedy could be tempted to harm themselves or others.

The contributing factor was as follows:
*   Removal of firearms in a stressful situation

---

c. You would not hesitate to prevent a friend or relative from drinking and driving. Do not hesitate to prevent the misuse of firearms by others.

8.3 Firearms Reported Lost, Missing or Stolen

a. Owners of restricted or prohibited firearms were required under the former *Criminal Code* to report the loss or theft of their restricted or prohibited firearms because it was only these that had to be registered. Because the *Firearms Act* now extends registration to all firearms, the requirement to report a loss or theft is also extended to non-restricted firearms. A person failing to report a firearm lost, missing or stolen to a peace officer, firearms officer, or chief firearms officer may be fined and/or jailed. The high number of firearms reported lost, missing or stolen each year may contribute to the intentional misuse of firearms. For further information on this subject, see Appendix H: Reporting Lost or Stolen Firearms, Licences, etc. at the back of this handbook or section 105 of Part III of the *Criminal Code*.

Example of An Accident Where Stolen Firearms Were Not Reported

A fifteen-year old boy stole six firearms from a man's house. Out of fear, the man did not immediately report his firearms missing because they were improperly stored in a closet without a secure locking device. The next day, at the time of reporting, he was unaware that, only four hours earlier, the fifteen-year old boy had loaded one of his firearms, pointed the firearm at himself in jest, discharged the firearm, and killed himself. Three of the firearms remain missing, and police fear that they are on the street.

The contributing factors were as follows:

- Firearms not locked or stored securely
- Failure to immediately report the loss of firearms
- Careless handling of a firearm

8.4 Secure Storage

a. Secure firearm storage is the best way to limit theft and deliberate misuse of firearms. It should not be easy for unauthorized users to get firearms and ammunition.

b. Do not leave the key or combination to the firearm storage area or container lying around. Do not give them out to others. Also, do not let it become widely known that you have firearms.

c. Locking up firearms and ammunition is important and, in many cases, required by law.

d. Make access to firearms and ammunition difficult. Many suicides and homicides arise from sudden impulses. If firearms and ammunition are difficult to get, there may be a delay in acting on the impulse to do harm. This delay may be enough to make the impulse decrease or go away.

e. Secure storage of firearms and ammunition may act as a deterrent to easy theft by criminals. **Remember: you are responsible for your firearms 24 hours a day.** This is both a legal and a moral responsibility. It is wise to store them safely and securely when you are not physically in control of them. This may cause some inconvenience, but it may also save a person from death or serious injury.

Please refer to Section 9 – SAFE STORAGE, DISPLAY, TRANSPORTATION & HANDLING OF NON-RESTRICTED FIREARMS.

⚠ **Carelessly stored firearms may be misused.**

8.5 Unintentional Misuse of Firearms

a. Most firearm accidents happen because of one or more of the following reasons:

- Unauthorized access or improper storage

- Lack of control of muzzle direction

- Careless or ignorant use

- Accidental firing

- Users who are not qualified

- Aiming or firing at the wrong target

- Using the wrong ammunition

- Lack of knowledge about firearms

 **Follow the Vital Four ACTS.**

b. Improper storage of firearms may lead to tragedy, if firearms get into the hands of unqualified or unauthorized persons.

Examples of Accidents

1. A rifle had been left loaded and within easy reach. A child started playing with it. A parent grabbed the rifle by the barrel. He pulled it away from the child. The rifle fired and the parent was wounded.

2. Two young children were playing in their home. They found a shotgun in the bedroom closet. One was killed when the shotgun fired.

The contributing factors were as follows:
- Improper storage of a firearm
- Unsafe muzzle direction
- Failure to teach firearm awareness to family members

---

c. Most accidents involve a muzzle being pointed at the holder of the firearm or someone else. The firearm is accidentally fired, because of one of the following reasons:

- Shooters have their finger in the trigger guard and on the trigger before they are absolutely ready to shoot; or

- Some other object accidentally pushes on or presses the trigger.

Examples of Accidents

3. A boy was carrying his rifle loaded, cocked and ready to fire. He had the trigger portion under his armpit. The rifle fired when he moved his arm. Another hunter was wounded.

4. A hunter and his brother were crawling through dense bush. The hunter had a loaded and cocked rifle. The rifle caught on a bush and accidentally fired. The brother was wounded.

The contributing factors were as follows:

- Unsafe muzzle direction or control

- Carrying a loaded and cocked firearm

---

d. Firearm accidents occur while getting in or out of a vehicle with a loaded firearm.

Examples of Accidents

5. In one case, a man propped his loaded firearm against a car. It fell and fired. The bullet ricocheted from the roof of the car. The person inside was hit.

6. A woman was getting out of a pick-up truck. As she did so, she pulled a shotgun towards herself by the barrel. The trigger caught on the seat and the shotgun fired. The woman was killed.

The contributing factors were as follows:

- Unsafe muzzle direction

- Loading a firearm before being ready to fire

- Careless handling of a firearm around vehicles

---

e. Many firearm accidents happen during loading and unloading.

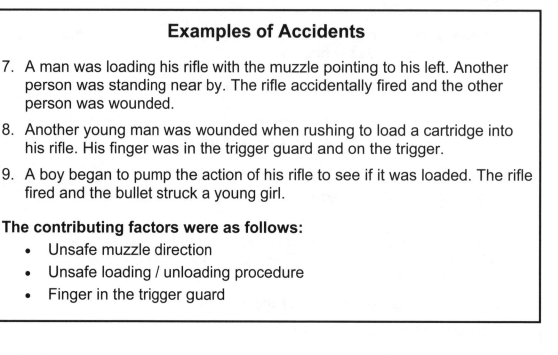

Examples of Accidents

7. A man was loading his rifle with the muzzle pointing to his left. Another person was standing near by. The rifle accidentally fired and the other person was wounded.

8. Another young man was wounded when rushing to load a cartridge into his rifle. His finger was in the trigger guard and on the trigger.

9. A boy began to pump the action of his rifle to see if it was loaded. The rifle fired and the bullet struck a young girl.

The contributing factors were as follows:
- Unsafe muzzle direction
- Unsafe loading / unloading procedure
- Finger in the trigger guard

f. Climbing or jumping over obstacles while carrying a loaded firearm may cause shooting injuries.

Examples of Accidents

10. A young woman crossed over a fence while holding a loaded firearm. Her rifle accidentally caught on the fence. It fired and she was wounded.

11. A man tossed his firearm over a small ditch he wanted to cross. As the firearm hit the ground, it fired. He was seriously wounded.

The contributing factors were as follows:
- Unsafe muzzle direction
- Crossing obstacles with a loaded firearm
- Crossing obstacles in an unsafe manner

g. Accidents can happen when the wrong ammunition is used.

Examples of Accidents

12. A hunter was carrying a mix of different shotgun shells in his pocket. He accidentally loaded a 20-gauge shell into his 12-gauge shotgun. When it did not fire, he inserted a 12-gauge shell behind the first shell and fired. The barrel burst and injured the shooter's face.

13. A box of ammunition purchased at a store contained a similar but incorrect cartridge. It had probably been switched accidentally by a previous customer. When the firearm was fired, the barrel burst and injured the shooter's hands.

The contributing factors were as follows:

- Failure to match the data stamp on the firearm with the head stamp on the cartridge
- Carrying and using the wrong ammunition

8.6 Table 11 - Firearm Hazards and Precautions

a. Table 11 summarizes some firearm hazards and appropriate precautions to take.

Table 11. Firearm Hazards and Precautions

Hazard	Precautions
Access by unqualified or unauthorized users	• Disable action before storage or transport (or use trigger or cable lock) • Store firearms in a safely locked cabinet or container, out of view • Store ammunition separately and out of view • Supervise unqualified users
Accidental firing	• Control muzzle direction at all times • Unload firearm when not in immediate use • Open action when handling • Keep finger off trigger and out of the trigger guard except when firing • Safety ON • No horseplay • A malfunctioning firearm may result in accidental discharge • Ensure your firearm is well maintained and regularly serviced
Wrong ammunition	• Carry only correct ammunition • Check ammunition against firearm data stamp • Use proper ammunition for target and conditions • If re-loading, follow correct procedures • Improperly loaded ammunition can cause a firearm accident • Ensure you know how to load correctly
Ricochets	• Be extra cautious when shooting at or towards flat or hard surfaces • Check area near or behind target before firing • Be extra cautious when shooting at or towards water
Wrong target	• Identify target before firing • Know what is behind target • Make sure the backstop is adequate

8.7 Social Responsibilities and Ethics

a. As a firearms user, you have certain legal obligations to the community at large. In some cases, however, sticking to the letter of the law is not enough. The spirit of the law must also be followed. The welfare and well being of your fellow citizens must come first.

b. Below are some moral and social rules. They must be part of the code of ethics for anyone possessing firearms.

1. **Store all firearms and ammunition properly.** Keep your firearms and ammunition properly secured and out of sight.

2. **Explain firearms safety to all family members**. Everyone in a home where firearms are kept should know the safety rules. Firearms are no different than dangerous tools or poisons in the home. Proper use and handling of firearms and ammunition must be taught to the entire family. The key or combination number to secure locking devices should be kept away from and out of the reach of children and unauthorized adults.

3. **Remove firearms from situations of potential violence.** You may become aware of a situation where violence or tragedy could occur. In such cases, it is wise to go beyond the safe storage of firearms. Completely remove firearms that may be present. If this is not possible, at least notify the police of the situation.

4. **Act sensibly and carefully while around firearms.** Always pay close attention to what you and others around you are doing. Make sure that everyone is acting safely and responsibly.

5. **Never consume drugs or alcoholic beverages when around firearms**. Do not go shooting with anyone who has. Alcohol and drugs can affect your mental or physical reactions. Both prescription and non-prescription drugs can affect your alertness, senses and balance. Some types of allergy medicines are a good example. Always stay fully alert when around firearms.

6. **Always get permission before shooting on someone else's property**. Make sure you are welcome and permitted before you shoot anywhere. Do this whether the land belongs to the crown, to a local club, or a private citizen. Make sure that you can shoot there safely. For example, someone else may be shooting there at the same time.

7. **Have your eyesight checked regularly.** Shooting requires good vision for target identification and accuracy. Be sure of your target and beyond.

8. **Maintain your firearm in good working order**. If required, have a qualified gunsmith service your firearm.

9. **Avoid firing near any buildings or roads**. Respect the rights of others to safe travel and undisturbed use of their property. Only shoot near buildings with authorized permission, and only if it is legal and safe.

10. **Know and respect firearms regulations and local by-laws**. Some of these are listed in section 8.9.

11. **Wear safety equipment**. Encourage others to do the same. Safety equipment may include, but should not be limited to, eye and hearing protection, gloves, caps, and proper clothing.

8.8 Table 12 - Social Responsibilities of a Firearm User

Table 12. Social Responsibilities of a Firearm User

Social Responsibilities of a Firearms User (summary of)
1. Store all firearms and ammunition properly.   2. Explain firearms safety to all family members.   3. Remove firearms from situations of potential violence.   4. Act sensibly and carefully while around firearms.   5. Never consume drugs or alcoholic beverages when around firearms.   6. Always get permission before shooting on someone else's property.   7. Have your eyesight checked regularly.   8. Maintain your firearm in good working order.   9. Avoid firing near any buildings or roads.   10. Know and respect firearms regulations and local by-laws.   11. Wear safety equipment.

8.9 Legal Responsibilities

a. As a firearm owner and user, you have legal as well as social responsibilities. These responsibilities are laid down in federal, provincial/territorial and municipal laws and regulations. Table 13 describes a few of the regulations that come from each level of government.

Table 13. Some Legal Responsibilities of a Firearms User

Some Legal Responsibilities of a Firearms User	
Government Level	**Example of Law or Regulation**
Federal (e.g. *Firearms Act* and its *Regulations, Criminal Code*)	• All firearm owners need a valid licence, and all firearms must be registered. • If you are the holder of a valid Firearms Licence, you must inform the RCMP/CAFC when you change your address. • Persons holding a valid Possession Only Licence (POL) may borrow the same class of firearms that he/she is licenced to own. Persons holding a valid Possession and Acquisition Licence may borrow, buy, inherit or otherwise acquire the same class of firearm that he/she is licenced to own.
Provincial/Territorial (e.g. *Game, Fish and Wildlife Acts*)	• Some provinces/territories may require anyone who hunts with a non-restricted firearm to wear blaze orange clothing. • Some restrict shooting across or within a certain distance of roads or dwellings. • Some provincial/territorial laws may limit your use of motorized vehicles while hunting or shooting.
Municipal/County/Local (e.g. Noise, Nuisance, Zoning, By-laws)	• Some municipalities or counties may not allow firing of a firearm under any circumstances within their boundaries. • Some will regulate firing times and/or closeness to dwellings.

8.10 Other Duties of Firearm Owners and Users

a. Automobile drivers are expected to know the rules of the road. They are also required to know any driving related laws and regulations.

b. A firearm owner/user must also keep informed about the laws and regulations affecting the use of firearms and ammunition.

c. Going beyond what the regulations require will increase your safety. Some suggestions are listed below:

   •   Keep an inventory of your firearms. Also keep any supporting documents such as photographs and owner's manuals. Store these documents in a safe place. This will help you describe any firearms that may be stolen or lost. It will also be easier for you to find your owner's manual and records of service or repair.

   •   Keep informed. Changes may occur in laws and regulations from time to time. This can happen at any level, whether at the federal, provincial/territorial or municipal.

   •   Avoid advertising about the firearms in your home. You may be inviting theft.

d. You can be prosecuted if you ignore regulations that apply to firearm owners and users.

 Every person commits an offence who, without lawful excuse, points a firearm at another person, whether the firearm is loaded or unloaded, and is:

1. **guilty of an indictable offence and liable to imprisonment for a term not exceeding five years; or**

2. **guilty of an offence punishable on summary conviction (a fine of $2,000 and/or six months' imprisonment).**

Reference: Subsections 87(1) and (2) of Part III of the *Criminal Code*

Every person who stores, displays transports or handles any firearm in a manner contrary to the *Storage, Display, Transportation and Handling of Firearms by Individuals Regulations* is:

1. **guilty of an indictable offence and liable to imprisonment,**

    -   **in the case of a first offence, for a term not exceeding two years, and**
    -   **in the case of a second or subsequent offence, for a term not exceeding five years; or**

2. **guilty of an offence punishable on summary conviction (a fine of $2,000 and/or six months' imprisonment).**

Reference: Subsections 86(2) and (3) of Part III of the *Criminal Code*

e. Not all firearms laws can be included in this handbook. If you are in any doubt about the regulations or if you need more information, you can take the following steps:

    -   Contact a firearms officer.

    -   Obtain a copy of the federal legislation and regulations from your Chief Firearms Officer.

f. You can also get information about provincial/territorial and municipal laws and regulations from your local police station or wildlife agency.

8.11 Review Questions

1. Suicide and homicide are the leading causes of firearms-related deaths and injuries. How may this type of firearms misuse be reduced?

2. List three frequent contributing factors that may lead to firearm accidents.

3. List five examples of socially responsible behaviors for a firearms user.

NOTES:

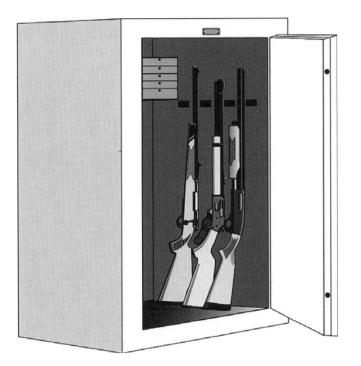

Section 9

SAFE STORAGE, DISPLAY, TRANSPORTATION & HANDLING OF NON-RESTRICTED FIREARMS

9 - SAFE STORAGE, DISPLAY, TRANSPORTATION AND HANDLING OF NON-RESTRICTED FIREARMS

9.1 Classes of Firearms

9.1.0 Overview

a. See Tables 14, 15 & 16, which provide a brief description of each class of firearms. For legal references, however, please refer to the *Firearms Act* and its *Regulations*, and Part III of the *Criminal Code*.

9.1.1 Table 14 - Non-Restricted Firearms

Table 14. Non-Restricted Firearms

Non-Restricted Firearms (classes of firearms)
Generally, firearms commonly used for hunting or sporting purposes such as target shooting are included in this class. The following are examples of non-restricted firearms: • Rifles • Shotguns

9.1.2 Table 15 - Restricted Firearms

Table 15. Restricted firearms

Restricted Firearms (classes of firearms)
In general, individuals may possess restricted firearms for one or more of the following reasons: lawful profession or occupation, target practice or competition, as part of a gun collection or, in some rare cases, for the protection of life. The following are examples of restricted firearms: • A handgun which is not a prohibited firearm; • A firearm that is not a prohibited firearm, has a barrel less than 470 mm (18½ in.) in length, and discharges centre-fire ammunition in a semi-automatic manner. • A firearm that is designed or adapted to be fired when reduced to a length of less than 660 mm (26 in.) by folding, telescoping or otherwise • A firearm of any kind that is prescribed by regulation to be a restricted firearm

It must be noted that some rifles and shotguns are considered restricted or prohibited. Persons wishing to acquire such firearms should contact a firearms officer for further information.

9.1.3 Table 16 - Prohibited Firearms

Table 16. Prohibited Firearms

Prohibited Firearms (classes of firearms)
In general, individuals cannot acquire the types of firearms that fall into the prohibited class. Depending on the nature of their duties, employees of businesses and carriers, and public officers (police or peace officer, firearms officer, prescribed employee of a federal, provincial or municipal government) may possess prohibited firearms. The following are examples of prohibited firearms: • Handguns with a barrel length equal to or less than 105 mm (4⅛ in.) • Handguns designed or adapted to discharge a 25- or 32-calibre cartridge (any of the above-noted handguns are not prohibited firearms if they are used in competitions governed by the rules of the International Shooting Union and prescribed by regulation) • "Sawed-off" rifles or "sawed-off" shotguns less than 660 mm (26 in.) in length • "Sawed-off" rifles or "sawed-off" shotguns 660 mm (26 in.) or greater in length and have barrel lengths of less than 457 mm (18 in.) • An automatic firearm • Any firearm that is prescribed by regulation to be a prohibited firearm

9.2 Ammunition

9.2.0 Overview

Ammunition, Prohibited Ammunition and Prohibited Devices

a. Ammunition, prohibited ammunition and prohibited devices are defined in Part III of the Criminal Code. The following tables (17, 18 & 19) provide a brief description of each group. For a complete description, consult the *Criminal Code of Canada.*

Table 17. Ammunition

Ammunition
Ammunition is a cartridge containing a projectile designed to be discharged from a firearm. This includes caseless cartridges and shot shells.

9.2.1 Table 18 - Prohibited Ammunition

Table 18. Prohibited Ammunition

Prohibited Ammunition
Individuals cannot acquire prohibited ammunition. Depending on the nature of their duties, employees of businesses and carriers, and public officers (police or peace officer, firearms officer, prescribed employee of a federal, provincial or municipal government) may possess prohibited ammunition. The following are examples of ammunition prescribed by regulation as prohibited *ammunition:* • Any cartridge that can be fired from a commonly available semi-automatic handgun or revolver and has a projectile specifically designed to penetrate body armour • Any projectile that can ignite on impact, is made to be used in or with a cartridge, and is not more than 15 mm (⅝ in.) in diameter • Any projectile that can explode on impact, is made to be used in or with a cartridge, and is not more than 15 mm (⅝ in.) in diameter • Any cartridge that can be fired from a shotgun and contains projectiles, known as flechettes, or any similar projectiles

9.2.2 Table 19 - Prohibited Devices

Table 19. Prohibited Devices

Prohibited Devices
Individuals cannot acquire prohibited devices. Prohibited devices are regulated under the *Criminal Code*. Depending on the nature of their duties, employees of businesses and carriers, and public officers (police or peace officer, firearms officer, prescribed employee of a federal, provincial or municipal government) may possess prohibited devices. The following are examples of prohibited devices: • Any part of a weapon or accessory of a weapon that is prescribed by regulation to be a prohibited device • A handgun barrel that is equal to or less than 105 mm (4⅛ in.) in length (does not include any handgun barrel that is used in competitions governed by the rules of the *International Shooting Union* and prescribed by regulation) • A device designed to muffle or stop the sound of a firearm (silencers) • A cartridge magazine prescribed by regulation to be a prohibited device • Replica firearms

Refer to the appropriate sections of the *Firearms Act and Regulations* for detailed requirements relating to the storage, display, transportation and handling of non-restricted firearms.

a. **Remember, you are responsible for your firearms 24 hours a day.** Anyone who owns or uses a firearm must meet safe storage, display, transportation and handling requirements. These requirements are set out in the *Storage, Display, Transportation and Handling of Firearms by Individuals Regulations.* All of these are described in this section.

b. Firearms owners and users should always assume that anyone untrained in the safe handling and use of firearms does not know how to handle firearms safely. Fatal incidents or serious accidents could occur from unauthorized access, especially where children are concerned. To prevent this, always store, display, transport and handle firearms and ammunition in accordance with the Regulations.

c. **Remember the law requires that all firearms must be unloaded** except when actually in use.

9.3 Storage

a. A non-restricted firearm may be stored only under the following conditions:

- It is unloaded, **and**

    - Rendered inoperable by using a secure locking device **or**

    - By removing the bolt or bolt-carrier **or**

    - Stored in a securely locked container, receptacle, or room that cannot be easily broken open or into (see Figure 73); **and**

- Not within easy access to ammunition, unless the ammunition is stored, together with or separately from the firearm, in a securely locked container or receptacle that cannot be easily broken open or into.

 Keep in mind that storing ammunition in an unvented container may create an explosive hazard during a fire.

b. In areas where it is legal to discharge a firearm, a non-restricted firearm used for predator control may be stored temporarily unlocked, and out in the open, as long as it is unloaded, and not readily accessible to ammunition.

c. In a remote area where hunting might reasonably occur, a non-restricted firearm may be stored unlocked, out in the open and accessible to ammunition as long as the firearm is unloaded.

Figure 73. Storage vault

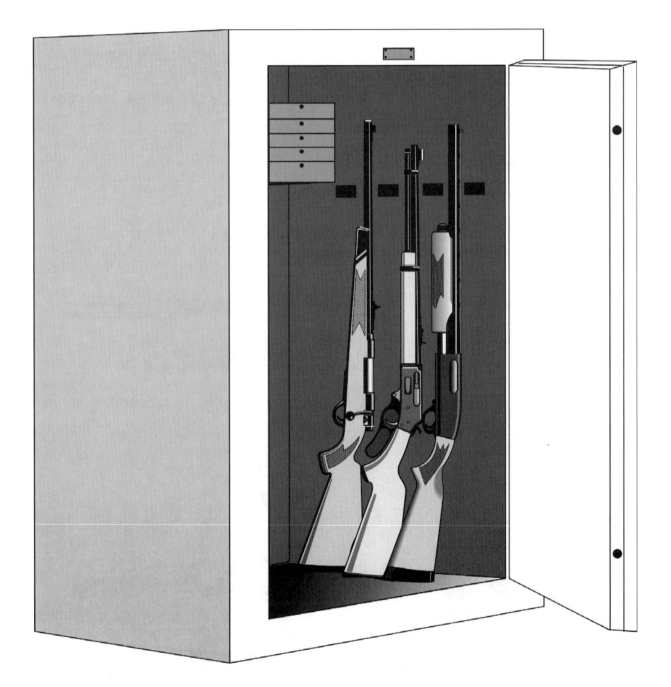

9.4 Display

a. A non-restricted firearm may be displayed only under the following conditions:

- Unloaded, **and**
  - Rendered inoperable by using a secure locking device (see Figures 74 & 75) **or**
  - Stored in a securely locked container, receptacle or room that cannot be easily broken open or into; **and**
- Not displayed with and not within easy access to ammunition that can be discharged from it.

Figure 74. Cable and trigger locks

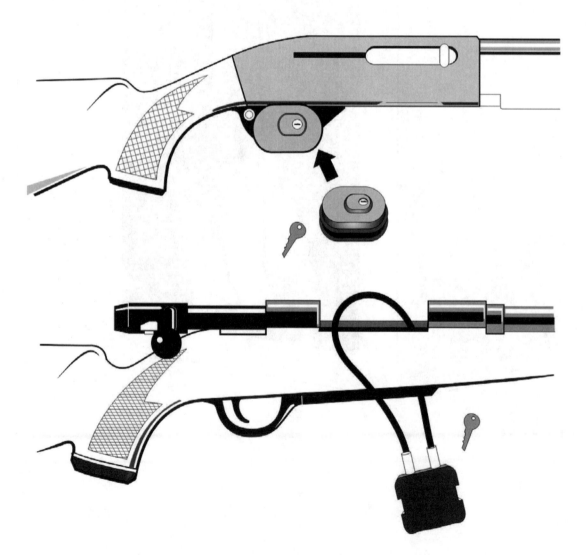

Figure 75. Display

9.5 Transportation

a. A non-restricted firearm must be transported unloaded.

b. However, loaded-muzzleloading firearms may be transported between hunting sites if the percussion cap or flint is removed, subject to provincial/territorial regulations.

c. You may leave a non-restricted firearm in an unattended vehicle if it is unloaded and placed in a locked trunk or a similar compartment of the vehicle.

d. If the unattended vehicle does not have a trunk or a similar compartment, lock the vehicle or the part of the vehicle that contains the non-restricted firearm and leave the non-restricted firearm inside, unloaded and out of sight.

e. In a remote area when hunting might reasonably occur, you may leave a non-restricted firearm in an unattended vehicle that has no trunk or compartment that can be locked (e.g. canoe, kamik, snowmobile), if it is out of sight. The non-restricted firearm must be unloaded and rendered inoperable by a secure locking device unless you require it for predator control.

f. If you live in a rural area and need reasonable access to your non-restricted firearm for predator control, you may be exempted from some of the storage and transportation requirements. Check with a local wildlife or conservation officer to confirm that provincial or municipal laws allow storage on a temporary basis.

If you want to transport firearms on an aircraft, you should first contact the air carrier. They will provide information on their regulations and requirements.

Every person who stores, displays, transports or handles any firearm in a manner contrary to the *Storage, Display, Transportation and Handling of Firearms by Individuals Regulations* is:

1. **guilty of an indictable offence and liable to imprisonment,**

    • **in the case of a first offence, for a term not exceeding two years, and**

    • **in the case of a second or subsequent offence, for a term not exceeding five years; or**

2. **guilty of an offence punishable on summary conviction (a fine of $2,000 and/or six months' imprisonment).**

Reference: Subsections 86(2) and (3) of Part III of the *Criminal Code*

9.6 Handling

a. Before obtaining a firearm, think about how you will carry it home and where you will keep it. Remember, when you leave the seller or dealer's shop, you will be carrying your firearm in a public place. It is recommended that all firearms be carried in a case or container to avoid display in public (see fig. 76).

b. There are locations where having or discharging a firearm violates federal or provincial/territorial Acts and Regulations, or municipal bylaws. It may also be an offence to load or handle firearms in these places. You may load a firearm or handle a loaded firearm only in a place where it is lawful to discharge it.

 **Only load a firearm when you intend to use it, and only in an area where it can be safely and legally discharged.**

Figure 76. Case

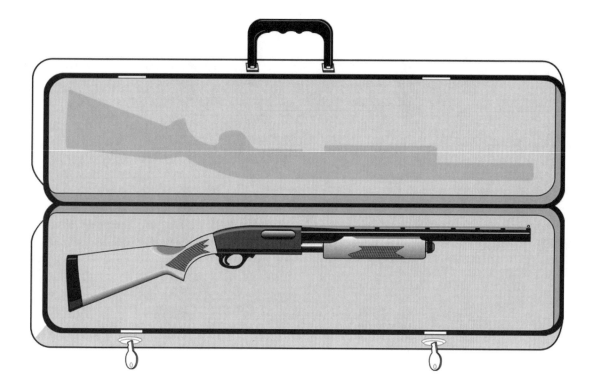

Every person commits an offence who, without lawful excuse, points a firearm at another person, whether the firearm is loaded or unloaded, and is:

1. guilty of an indictable offence and liable to imprisonment for a term not exceeding five years; or

2. guilty of an offence punishable on summary conviction (a fine of $2,000 and/or six months' imprisonment).

Reference: Subsections 87(1) and (2) of Part III of the *Criminal Code*

9.7 Table 20 - The Vital Four ACTS

Table 20. The Vital Four ACTS of Firearm Safety

	The Vital Four ACTS of Firearm Safety
☞	**Assume every firearm is loaded.** • Regard any firearm as a potential danger.
☞	**Control the muzzle direction at all times.** • Identify the safest available muzzle direction. • Keep the firearm pointed in the safest available direction. • The muzzle of a firearm should not be pointed towards yourself or any other person.
☞	**Trigger finger must be kept off the trigger and out of the trigger guard.** • Resist the temptation to put your finger on the trigger or inside the trigger guard when you pick up a firearm. • Accidental discharge is far more likely to occur if your finger is on the trigger or inside the trigger guard.
☞	**See that the firearm is unloaded - PROVE it safe.** • Do not handle the firearm unless you can properly **PROVE** it safely. • Check to see that both chamber and magazine are empty. Do this every time you handle a firearm, for any reason. • Pass or accept only open and unloaded firearms. This is an important habit to develop.

9.8 PROVE Safe

PROVE it safe:

- **P**oint the firearm in the safest available direction.

- **R**emove all ammunition.

- **O**bserve the chamber.

- **V**erify the feeding path.

- **E**xamine the bore for obstructions.

The firearm is now unloaded and safe until it leaves the direct control of the person who unloaded and PROVEd it safe.

9.9 Review Questions

1. Can firearms be stored next to ammunition when both are in a locked container? Explain.

2. Between hunting sites, must all non-restricted firearms be transported unloaded? Explain why.

3. Can a firearm be left in a vehicle that does not have a trunk? Explain.

4. What are the consequences of contravening the *Storage, Display, Transportation and Handling of Firearms by Individuals Regulations?*

NOTES:

APPENDIXES

Appendix A: Overview

These appendixes are provided for general information purposes only. The information contained in this section may be additional to that contained in the course. Information contained in this section will not form part of the written or practical tests.

For legal references, please refer to the actual legislation, namely the *Firearms Act* and its Regulations, and Part III of the *Criminal Code*.

Appendix B: Antique Firearms

An antique firearm refers to any firearm manufactured before 1898 that was not designed or redesigned to discharge rim-fire or centre-fire ammunition, plus any other firearm specifically identified as an antique by Regulations. Owners of antique firearms do not need to have a firearms licence or a registration certificate. There are also no restrictions on the transfer of antique firearms. However, antique firearms owners must comply with the requirements found in the *Storage, Display, Transportation and Handling of Firearms by Individuals Regulations.*

Source: Section 84, Part III of the *Criminal Code,* Paragraph 117(h), *Firearms Act*

Appendix C: Buying Ammunition

Any individual wishing to buy ammunition in Canada must have a valid Canadian firearms licence. (Non-residents must have either a confirmed declaration or a temporary borrowing licence to buy ammunition in Canada.)

Appendix D: Legal Definitions

The following definitions are taken from the *Firearms Act* and its *Regulations*, and Part III of the *Criminal Code*.

ammunition: A cartridge containing a projectile designed to be discharged from a firearm and, without restricting the generality of the foregoing, includes a caseless cartridge and a shot shell. (*munitions*)

antique firearm: (1) Any firearm manufactured before 1898 that was not designed to discharge rim-fire or centre-fire ammunition and that has not been redesigned to discharge such ammunition. (2) Any firearm that is prescribed to be an antique firearm. (*arme à feu historique*)

firearm: A barrelled weapon from which any shot, bullet or other projectile can be discharged and that is capable of causing serious bodily injury or death to a person, and includes any frame or receiver of such a barrelled weapon and anything that can be adapted for use as a firearm. (*arme à feu*)

handgun: A firearm that is designed, altered or intended to be aimed and fired by the action of one hand, whether or not it has been redesigned or subsequently altered to be aimed and fired by the action of both hands. (*arme de poing*)

non-restricted firearm: A firearm that is neither a prohibited firearm nor a restricted firearm. (*arme à feu sans restrictions*)

prohibited ammunition: Ammunition, or a projectile of any kind, that is prescribed to be prohibited ammunition. (*munitions prohibées*)

prohibited device: (1) Any component or part of a weapon, or any accessory for use with a weapon, that is prescribed to be a prohibited device. (2) A handgun barrel that is equal to or less than 105 mm in length, but does not include any such handgun barrel that is prescribed, where the handgun barrel is for use in international sporting competitions governed by the rules of the International Shooting Union. (3) A device or contrivance designed or intended to muffle or stop the sound or report of a firearm. (4) A cartridge magazine that is prescribed to be a prohibited device. (5) Replica firearm. (*dispositif prohibé*)

prohibited firearm: (1) A handgun that has a barrel equal to or less than 105 mm in length; or is designed or adapted to discharge a 25- or 32-calibre cartridge, but does not include any such handgun that is prescribed, where the handgun is for use in international sporting competitions governed by the rules of the International Shooting Union. (2) A firearm that is adapted from a rifle or shotgun, whether by sawing, cutting or any other alteration, and that, as so adapted, is less than 660 mm in length; or is 660 mm or greater in length and has a barrel less than 457 mm in length. (3) An automatic firearm, whether or not it has been altered to discharge only one projectile with one pressure of the trigger. (4) Any firearm that is prescribed to be a prohibited firearm. (*arme à feu prohibée*)

replica firearm: Any device that is designed or intended to exactly resemble, or to resemble with near precision, a firearm, and that itself is not a firearm, but does not include any such device that is designed or intended to exactly resemble, or to resemble with near precision, an antique firearm. (*réplique*)

restricted firearm: (1) A handgun that is not a prohibited firearm. (2) A firearm that is not a prohibited firearm; has a barrel less than 470 mm in length; and is capable of discharging centre-fire ammunition in a semi-automatic manner. (3) A firearm that is designed or adapted to be fired when reduced to a length of less than 660 mm by folding, telescoping or otherwise. (4) A firearm of any other kind that is prescribed to be a restricted firearm. (*arme à feu à autorisation restreinte*)

secure locking device: A device that can only be opened or released by the use of an electronic, magnetic or mechanical key or by setting the device in accordance with an alphabetical or numerical combination; and that, when applied to a firearm, prevents the firearm from being discharged. (*dispositif de verrouillage sécuritaire*)

unattended: In respect of a vehicle, means that the vehicle is not under the direct and immediate supervision of a person who is 18 years of age or older or to whom a licence has been issued under the Act. (*non surveillé*)

unloaded: In respect of a firearm, means that any propellant, projectile or cartridge that can be discharged from the firearm is not contained in the breech or firing chamber of the firearm nor in the cartridge magazine attached to or inserted into the firearm. (*non chargée*)

vehicle: Any conveyance that is used for transportation by water, land or air. (*véhicule*)

Appendix E: Firearms Licences

Under the Firearms Act anyone wishing to possess, borrow, buy, inherit or otherwise acquire firearms must have a valid Firearms Licence.

The Firearms Act and Firearms Licences Regulations set out the following types of individual firearms licences:

- Possession Only Licence

- Possession and Acquisition Licence

- Minors Possession Licence

- Non-resident Sixty-day Possession Licence (Borrowed Firearms)

- Non-resident Firearm Declaration (Confirmation of Importation of a Firearm by a Non-resident)

Requirements for obtaining firearms licences are the same across Canada. Most, if not all of these licences are available on-line on the CAFC Internet website at: www.cfc-cafc.gc.ca.

Possession Only Licence (POL)

This type of licence authorizes the continued possession of firearms already owned, but does not permit the acquiring of additional firearms. This licence is no longer available to new licence applicants. Existing POL holders may renew their licence as long as they continue to lawfully and continuously possess at least one firearm in the particular class.

Possession and Acquisition Licence (PAL)

This type of licence is required for anyone wishing to acquire firearms, whether for the first time or in addition to the firearms already owned. An individual must successfully complete the Canadian Firearms Safety Course and/or tests to obtain this licence for non-restricted firearms. To obtain this licence for restricted firearms and/or prohibited firearms an individual must also successfully complete the Canadian Restricted Firearms Safety Course and/or tests. There is a minimum 28-day waiting period for this licence, unless the applicant already holds a valid POL, PAL or Minors Possession Licence.

Appendix F: Personal Firearms Inventory (example)

MAKE:

MODEL:

SERIAL No.:

FIREARM IDENTIFICATION NUMBER:

MANUFACTURER:

BARREL LENGTH:

CALIBRE/GAUGE:

REGISTRATION CERTIFICATE NUMBER:

PURCHASED FROM:

DATE OF PURCHASE:

VALUE:

DISTINGUISHING MARKS:

ACCESSORIES (case, grips, etc.):

Appendix G: Replica Firearms

A replica firearm is designed or intended to exactly, or almost exactly, resemble a firearm, but itself is not a firearm. Under Part III of the *Criminal Code*, a replica firearm is a prohibited device. Owners of replica firearms do not need to have a firearms licence or a registration certificate. However, replica firearms owners must comply with the transportation requirements found in the *Storage, Display, Transportation and Handling of Firearms by Individuals Regulations.*

Source: Section 84, Part III of the *Criminal Code*, Paragraph 117(i), *Firearms Act*

Appendix H: Reporting Lost or Stolen Firearms, Licences, etc.

Where a firearm or other weapon is lost or stolen, or a licence, registration certificate or authorization is lost or stolen—it must be reported.

A person commits an offence if after having lost a firearm, a prohibited weapon, a restricted weapon, a prohibited device, any prohibited ammunition, an authorization, a licence or a registration certificate, or having had it stolen, does not report the loss or theft with reasonable dispatch to a peace officer, firearms officer, or Chief Firearms Officer.

Similarly, a person commits an offence, if on finding a firearm, a prohibited weapon, a restricted weapon, a prohibited device, or any prohibited ammunition, does not report the find, or deliver the item, with reasonable dispatch to a peace officer, firearms officer, or Chief Firearms Officer. This offence does not extend to documents, specifically an authorization, a licence or a registration certificate.

Commission of either offence is punishable on summary conviction or by indictment.

Source: Section 105, Part III of the *Criminal Code.*

Appendix I: Visual Range Signals and Devices

Flags or Signs: Typically a red flag flown at or near the entrance to the property. It serves to warn people that live fire may occur at any time and that shooters are actively using one or more ranges. Some clubs have individual "in use" flags for each range.

Down Range Activity Signals: Typically a red light, rope, or red flag at the entrance to the down range area. Red means stop! Do not go down range. A few clubs use a green flag or light to indicate it is safe to go down range. This display should NOT be visible from the shooting positions! Some ranges fly "down range" red flags to show it is NOT safe to discharge firearms; this is potentially confusing unless the flag cannot be seen by people in the down range area.

Shooting Line Activity Signals: Typically a red light, a red flashing light, a red flag, or a baffle clearly visible to the shooter when in the shooting position. Red means stop shooting! On some indoor ranges, the white lights that illuminate the firing line are dimmed and red illumination supplied. This display should NOT be positioned or used in a manner to be confused with the red signal at the entry to the down range area. Some ranges fly "down range" green flags to show that the range is safe for live fire; this is potentially confusing unless the flag cannot be seen by people in the down range area.

Appendix J: Gun Collector

The *Firearms Act* recognizes that collecting firearms is a legitimate reason for owning firearms. The rules on gun collecting apply to restricted firearms and to "grandfathered" prohibited handguns with barrel lengths of 105 mm or less, and of 25 and 32 calibre. In order to collect "grandfathered" handguns, an individual must have legally owned at least one such handgun on or before December 1, 1998. In order to qualify as a gun collector, a person must:

- have knowledge of the historical, technological or scientific characteristics of the firearms that are part of a collection;

- register his or her firearms as being part of a gun collection, and must agree to periodic inspections of the area where the collection is stored; and

- comply with such other requirements such as safe storage, display, handling and transportation standards, in addition to keeping records of the firearms that are part of a collection.

In addition, every five years, individuals will have to establish that they are gun collectors and that the firearms are kept for collection purposes.

Source: Section 30, *Firearms Act*

Appendix K: Transferring Firearms

Sections 22 and 23 of the *Firearms Act* set out a number of conditions that must be satisfied by both parties involved in the transfer of a firearm before the transfer is authorized. In addition, there are a number of conditions that apply in the *Conditions of Transferring Firearms and Other Weapons Regulations*. These obligations apply to each and every transfer of firearms, regardless of the class of firearm.

The following outlines the information that must be provided when individuals transfer (sell, barter, or give away) firearms.

Transferor's Obligations
An individual who wants to transfer a firearm must:

1. be reasonably sure that the transferee does not have a mental illness which would give rise to public safety concerns;

2. be reasonably sure that the transferee is not impaired by alcohol or drugs;

3. require the transferee to show a licence which authorizes the transferee to acquire and possess the particular class of firearm;

4. be satisfied that the licence shown authorizes the transferee to acquire and possess the particular class of firearm;

5. inform a Chief of Firearms Officer of the transfer and obtain his or her authorization;

6. ensure that the following conditions (subsection 2(1) of the *Conditions of Transferring Firearms and Other Weapons Regulations*) are complied with;

   - provide the Chief Firearms Officer with the transferor's and transferee's name and address;
   - provide the Chief Firearms Officer with the transferor's and transferee's licence numbers; and
   - inform the Chief Firearms Officer of the class of firearm being transferred.

Transferee's Obligations

In order for a transfer to be authorized, the individual to whom the firearms will be transferred must:

1. hold a possession and acquisition licence for the particular class of firearm;

2. ensure that a new registration certificate is issued by the Registrar;

3. for the transfer of restricted firearms and prohibited handguns (pre-December 1, 1998) only,

   - inform the Chief Firearms Officer why he or she needs to acquire the firearms (the protection of life, lawful profession or occupation, target practice or competition, or part of a gun collection);
   - if the transferee is acquiring the firearm to form part of a gun collection, he or she will have to provide the Chief Firearms Officer with:
     - information regarding his or her knowledge of characteristics which relate or distinguish the restricted firearms or handguns that he or she possesses;
     - signed consent to reasonably conducted periodic inspections of the area where the collection is kept; and
     - details of his or her knowledge of safe storage requirements for restricted firearms or prohibited handguns.

4. for the transfer of prohibited firearms only, provide the Chief Firearms Officer with the number of the registration certificate issued to him or her.

Before authorizing a transfer, the Chief Firearms Officer must determine whether or not the transfer will affect the safety of others. If the transfer is authorized, the Chief Firearms Officer will issue a unique transfer authorization number to both parties. Where transfers are completed by telephone, the transfer number provided to both parties will serve as a confirmation of the transfer and as a temporary registration certificate until a new registration certificate is sent in the mail.

Effective January 1, 2003, registration information will have to be verified by an authorized verifier. The transferor will be asked to provide evidence that the information concerning the firearm has been verified by an authorized verifier. Verification has to be done only once and the registration certificate will indicate whether or not the firearm data has been verified.

GLOSSARY

A

action: The moving parts of a firearm that load, fire, extract and eject ammunition.

action release: The part of a firearm that unlatches or opens the action to give access to the chamber.

airgun: A firearm that uses compressed air or carbon dioxide to propel a projectile.

ammunition: See under Appendix D: Legal Definitions.

antique firearm: See under Appendix D: Legal Definitions.

aperture sight: A rear sight with a hole for viewing the target. Also known as a peep sight.

automatic: An action that fires cartridges in rapid succession during one sustained pressure of the trigger.

B

ball:
a) A lead projectile fired by black powder firearms.
b) Full-metal jacket ammunition.

ballistics: The study of projectiles in flight and what affects them. This means the barrel, in flight and within the target, including trajectory, force, impact and penetration.

barrel: The metal tube of a firearm. The bullet, shot or projectile accelerates down it when the firearm is fired.

barrel length: The distance from the muzzle to the chamber, including the chamber itself. This measurement does not include accessories or barrel extensions like flash suppressors or muzzle brakes. The barrel length of a revolver is the distance from the muzzle to the breech end immediately in front of the cylinder.

BB gun: A type of air gun designed to use spherical steel BB pellets.

big bore: A rifle-shooting term that refers to centre-fire firearms or ammunition.

black powder: A finely ground powder, mainly used in muzzleloaders and antique cartridge firearms. The basic ingredients are salt-petre (potassium nitrate), charcoal (carbon) and sulphur.

blueing or bluing: An oxidation (rust) process applied to firearm metal parts. Controlled by applying oil that mixes with the nitrates used in the process. The oil prevents further rusting by sealing the metal. This gives the metal a blue-black colour that resulted in the name "bluing".

boat tail: The tapered rear end of some bullets, used to increase ballistic efficiency at long range.

bolt: A steel rod-like assembly that moves back and forth in an action, sealing the cartridge in the chamber during firing.

bolt action: For registration purposes, a repeating firearm that has a magazine and in which the breech bolt or closure device operates in line with the bore; manually operated by a permanent projection or handle attached to the bolt or closure device.

bolt face: The forward end of the bolt that supports the base of the cartridge.

bore: The inside of the barrel of a firearm excluding the chamber. The channel through which the bullet or other projectile is fired from the gun.

bore diameter: The measurement from one side of the bore to the other. See also **rifling; calibre.**

breech: The rear end of the barrel into which the ammunition is loaded. See also **chamber.**

breechblock: The part in the breech mechanism that locks the action against the firing of the cartridge.

breechloader: A firearm loaded through the breech.

buckshot: Large lead pellets used in shotgun shells.

bullet: A projectile designed to be fired from a rifled barrel.

butt: The rear end of a rifle or shotgun (the portion that rests against the shoulder.) In a handgun, the bottom part of the grip.

butt stock: In long guns, the part of the stock which extends from the receiver to the butt.

C

calibre: A measurement in metric or imperial units to describe the inside diameter of the barrel of a rifled firearm. Calibre is also used to describe the diameter of a projectile in a cartridge.

cap: See **percussion cap.**

carbine: A light-short-barrelled rifle.

cartridge: A complete unit of ammunition consisting of a case, primer, powder and a projectile. Modern cartridges are generally classified into two categories: centre-fire and rim-fire. See also **shell.**

cartridge magazine: A device or container from which ammunition may be fed into the firing chamber of
a firearm. Part 4 of the *Regulations Prescribing Certain Firearms and other Weapons, Components, and Parts of Weapons, Accessories, Cartridge Magazines, Ammunition and Projectiles as Prohibited or Restricted* sets out the limit for the number of cartridges permitted for different types of magazines. The two common types are box-type magazine and tubular-type magazine.

case: Also called casing. The container of a cartridge. It is usually of brass or other metal when used for rifles and handguns. When used for shotguns, it is usually of paper or plastic with a metal head, and is more often called a hull.

cease-fire:
a) As a verb - The command to stop shooting, unload firearms and step behind the cease-fire line.
b) As a noun - Time or period of range inactivity while targets are changed or other activities are conducted.

centre-fire: A cartridge with its primer located in the centre of the base of the case.

chainfiring: The term used to describe the dangerous result of not using grease over the balls used in a black powder revolver. When the primary cylinder is fired, lack of grease on the other cylinders may cause them to discharge before they are lined up with the barrel.

chamber:
a) The portion at the breech end of the barrel. The cartridge is placed in the chamber ready for firing. A revolver is multi chambered.
b) To place a cartridge in the barrel.

charge:
a) The amount, by weight, of the powder in a cartridge.
b) In the case of black powder, the amount, by volume, of the powder used.
c) To fill a magazine with cartridges.

Chief Firearms Officer: The person in authority in a province or territory responsible for licences, authorizations to transport, authorizations to carry and other functions related to the administration of the *Firearms Act* and its *Regulations.*

choke: Narrowing at the muzzle end of a shotgun barrel that determines the shot pattern.

cleaning kit: A set of specialized accessories used to clean and maintain a firearm.

clip: An incorrect term used to describe a magazine.

cock: To set the action into position for firing. On some firearms, the action has an intermediate position called half cock. On muzzleloading firearms, the cock holds the flint or match/wick.

coking: The burning of black powder residue with much heat and little smoke.

comb: The upper edge of a rifle or shotgun stock where the holder's cheek rests.

conical bullet: A cylindrical-shaped bullet with a cone shaped tip.

core: The part of a bullet that is covered by a jacket, i.e. the centre of a bullet.

corrosion: The gradual eating away of the metal parts of a firearm caused by rust or other chemical reactions.

crimp: The portion of a cartridge or shell case that is bent inward to hold the bullet or shot in place.

cross-bolt safety: A device that blocks the firing mechanism of a firearm.

cross-hairs: The sighting lines in a telescopic sight.

cylinder: The part of a revolver that rotates and in which chambers are bored to hold cartridges. It combines the functions of magazine, feed system and firing chamber.

cylinder bore: A shotgun barrel having the same diameter throughout, i.e. without choke. It is used to fire solid slugs.

D

dangerous range: The maximum distance at which a projectile will travel. See also **range.**

deactivated firearm: A deactivated firearm is one that has been rendered permanently inoperable. The standards for deactivated firearms are determined by the RCMP/CAFC.

dominant eye: See **master eye**.

double action: An action that cocks and fires with a complete pull of the trigger.

double action only: An action that cannot fire in a single action mode.

double action revolver: A revolver that both cocks and fires with a complete pull of the trigger.

double-barrel: A firearm with two barrels, either side-by-side or one over the other.

down range: The direction from the shooting position towards the target on a range. See also **range**.

dry firing: Firing of an unloaded firearm to practice handling and shooting techniques. This can damage some types of actions, particularly rim-fire.

dummy ammunition: Inactive ammunition used for practising handling of firearms. It has no primers or propellants. See also **live ammunition**.

E

effective range: The maximum distance for a shooter at which he or she can confidently hit the target. Also refers to the useful range of the projectile(s). See also **range.**

ejector: The mechanism that expels the cartridge or case from the firearm.

extraction: The removal of a cartridge or case from the chamber of a firearm.

F

feed: The action of moving a fresh cartridge into the chamber.

feeding path: The path a cartridge follows within an action.

field stripping: Taking apart a firearm for regular maintenance and cleaning.

firearm: See under Appendix D: Legal Definitions.

firing pin: The part of the breech mechanism that strikes the primer of the cartridge.

flash suppressor: Muzzle attachment designed to cool emergent gases and prevent or reduce muzzle flash.

flat-nosed bullet: A bullet with a flattened front end. It is used mainly in cartridges designed for rifles with tubular magazines.

flechette: A small dart stabilized by fins. It is encased in a discarding sabot (case) and loaded into a shotgun shell. Usually, one shell will contain a number of flechettes. This type of ammunition is prohibited.

flintlock: The gunlock of early firearms in which flint is struck against steel. This causes sparks to ignite the powder charge.

floor plate: The metal plate at the bottom of some cartridge magazines. (The floor plate is usually hinged at the front and held by a release spring located just ahead of the trigger guard.)

follow-through: Staying in the same position after squeezing the trigger or continuing the swing in firing at a moving target. This helps to shoot accurately.

follower: The part of a magazine between the spring and the ammunition. You must be able to see or feel the follower to know the magazine is empty. See also **magazine follower.**

forcing cone: In smooth-bore and revolver barrels, a cone that joins the chamber to the bore. It assists the passage of the projectile(s) into the bore. Also called a throat.

forearm/fore-stock: The forward part of a one or two-piece stock. It is sometimes called a slide on pump action firearms.

frizzen: The metal arm of a flintlock mechanism. The flint strikes the frizzen to create sparks in the flash pan. It is also called a battery.

full cock: The position of the hammer or striker when the firearm is ready to fire.

full metal jacket: A bullet with a jacket, usually of harder metal, encasing the core. It is also called a hard-point bullet. Used in ball ammunition.

G

gauge: The measurement of the diameter of a shotgun bore.

grain: A unit of weight (7,000 grains equal one pound) commonly used to measure the weight of ammunition components. Black powder and its substitutes are measured in grains by volume. Modern powders are measured by weight.

grip: The small portion of the stock gripped by the trigger hand.

grooves: See **rifling.**

H

half cock: A safety feature on some firearms. When the hammer is pulled back halfway, it cannot be fired by squeezing the trigger.

hammer: The part of the action that drives the firing pin forward.

handgun: See under Appendix D: Legal Definitions.

hangfire: A malfunction causing a delay in firing a cartridge after the firing pin has struck the primer.

high power: A term applied to the first smokeless-powder cartridges with velocities of approximately 609.6 m/s (2,000 ft./s).

high-power rifle: Generally, a firearm that uses centre-fire ammunition.

holding: The action of keeping the sights on the target while squeezing the trigger.

hollow point: A bullet with a hollow at the tip (nose) that makes it expand more on impact.

hull: The outer covering or casing of a shotgun shell.

I

No applicable entry.

J

jacket: The outer covering over the inner metal core of a bullet.

K

kick: See **recoil**.

L

lands: See **rifling.**

leading: Particles from shot or bullets that stick to the metal surface of the bore. This is due to heat or friction.

lever action:
a) An action operated by a lever located underneath it. (A secondary purpose of the lever is to serve as a trigger guard).
b) For registration purposes, a repeating firearm that has a magazine and a breech mechanism cycled by an external lever, usually below the receiver or frame.

line of sight: An imaginary straight line from the shooter's eye to the target; usually through the sights.

live ammunition: Ammunition containing primers and propellants capable of firing bullets or other projectiles.

load: To prepare a firearm for firing by inserting ammunition into it.

loading gate: The hinged cover over the opening through which cartridges are inserted into the magazine or chamber.

loading port: The opening through which cartridges are inserted into the magazine or chamber.

lock: The firing mechanism of a muzzleloader. In firearms that are loaded through the breech, the lock is both the firing mechanism and breech-sealing assembly.

long gun: Generic term used to describe rifles and shotguns.

M

magazine: See **cartridge magazine.**

magazine cut off: Disengages magazine feed from firearm.

magazine follower: Spring-loaded platform in a magazine. It pushes cartridges or shells to the feeding position. When checking that a firearm is completely unloaded, the magazine follower should be clearly in view. This is especially important with tubular magazines.

magazine release: A button or switch that allows for the removal of a magazine from the firearm.

magnum:
a) A cartridge or shell with a larger capacity or with a higher velocity than average (e.g. 3.5-inch Magnum shot shell, .300 Winchester Magnum rifle, .44 Remington Magnum handgun). Firearms that use magnum ammunition may also be called magnum.
b) A marketing term used by manufacturers which may or may not indicate greater power or range.

mainspring: A strong spring which activates the striker or hammer of a firearm.

malfunction: The failure of a firearm to work properly. This can be caused by a jam or stoppage, or a mechanical or structural failure.

master eye: The stronger eye; the eye through which a person usually views an object as when sighting a firearm.

match/wick: A long cord soaked in saltpetre, which burns slowly. Used to ignite powder in early firearms.

matchlock: A firearm action that uses a serpentine or S-shaped piece of metal to hold a smouldering match/wick. The burning match/wick contacts the priming powder in the pan to ignite the charge.

metallic cartridge: A cartridge with a metallic case. In contrast, early cartridge cases were made of linen, paper, etc.

mid-range: The point in the trajectory halfway between the muzzle and the target.

Mini-ball or Minie ball: A cylindrical-shaped bullet used in muzzleloaders. It has a pointed tip and a hollow base that spreads as it is fired.

misfire: The failure of a cartridge to fire after the firing pin has struck the primer. Do not confuse with hangfire, which is a delay in firing.

mushroom: The shape many soft-point bullets become when they expand upon impact.

musket: An early smooth-bore shoulder firearm.

muzzle: The opening at the end of the barrel from which the bullet or shot emerges.

muzzle brake: A device attached to the muzzle that softens the recoil of the firearm. Also known as a compensator.

muzzleloader: A firearm that is loaded through the muzzle.

N

non-restricted firearm: See under Appendix D: Legal Definitions.

O

open sight: A type of firearm sight, usually with a "V" or "U" notch in the rear sight. See also **sight.**

over-and-under: A firearm, usually a shotgun, with two barrels placed one over the other.

P

pan: The small container located on the side or top of a matchlock, wheel lock or flintlock firearm used to hold the priming powder.

patch:
a) A small piece of leather or cloth that is greased and placed around a bullet before ramming it down the barrel of a muzzleloader.
b) A piece of cloth drawn through the bore of a firearm to clean it.

patch box: A small compartment in the butt of a muzzleloader used to store patches or other small items.

pattern: Distribution of the shot in a shotgun charge. This is measured at a standard distance of 40 yd. and in a 30-inch circle.

peep sight: A rear sight with a hole through which the target is viewed. Also known as an aperture sight.

pellet: Small round projectiles loaded into shotgun shells. Usually referred to as shot. Also a lead projectile used in some air guns.

penetration: The depth that a projectile travels into a target before it stops.

percussion cap: A small metal explosive filled cup that is placed over the nipple of a percussion firearm.

pistol: A small hand-held firearm.

powder: The general term for any propellant used in firearms which burns upon ignition. The two major types are black powder (an explosive) and smokeless powder (a propellant).

powder burn: Charring caused by gunshot residue.

powder charge: The amount of powder by weight in the case of smokeless powder, and by volume, in the case of black powder.

prime: In the case of a black powder firearm, to place powder on the pan or percussion cap on the nipple. Also, to place a primer in a cartridge case.

primer: The overall term for the priming compound, cup and anvil which, when struck, ignites the powder charge.

primer pop: The sound of only the primer discharging due to no or grossly inadequate charge of powder in the cartridge.

prohibited ammunition: See under Appendix D: Legal Definitions.

prohibited device: See under Appendix D: Legal Definitions.

prohibited firearm: See under Appendix D: Legal Definitions.

projectile: A bullet or shot in flight after firing from a firearm.

propellant: The chemical substance which, when ignited, propels the projectile. Also called powder.

pull-through: The cord used to pull a bore brush or cleaning patch through the bore of a firearm.

pump action:
a) An action that is operated by moving the fore-end in a motion parallel to the bore.
b) For registration purposes, a repeating firearm that has a magazine and is manually set in motion usually parallel to the barrel; also called slide action or trombone action.

Q

No applicable entry.

R

ramrod: A wood or metal rod used to push the patch and bullet down the barrel of a muzzleloader.

range:
a) The distance travelled by a projectile from firearm to target.
b) A projectile's maximum travelling distance.
c) An area or facility designed for the safe shooting of firearms.
d) Dangerous range: the maximum distance at which a projectile will travel.
e) Effective range: the greatest distance a projectile will travel with accuracy.

receiver: A firearm's metal frame that generally contains the breech, locking and loading mechanisms. Normally the serial number is on the receiver. Also called the frame.

recoil: The backward movement of a firearm when it is fired. Also called kick.

replica firearm: See under Appendix D: Legal Definitions.

restricted firearm: See under Appendix D: Legal Definitions.

revolver:
a) A repeating handgun that has a revolving cylinder with a series of chambers. The cylinder may revolve in either direction, depending on the manufacturer.
b For registration purposes, a firearm, usually a handgun, that has a revolving cylinder with a series of chambers, and is discharged successively by the same firing mechanism. The chamber may revolve in either direction depending on the manufacturer.

revolving action: An action with a revolving cylinder containing a number of cartridge chambers. One chamber at a time lines up with the barrel.

ricochet: The redirection of a projectile after impact, usually with a hard surface. For example, a bullet bouncing off a rock.

rifle: A shoulder firearm with a rifled bore. Designed to fire one projectile at a time. See also **rifling.**

rifled slug: A large, single projectile with spiral grooves used in shotguns.

rifling: Spiral grooves inside the barrel. Rifling causes the bullet to spin, increasing its accuracy and range. The depressed portions of the rifling are called grooves and the raised portions are called lands.

rim: The edge on the base of a cartridge case. The rim is the part of the case that the extractor grips to remove the cartridge from the chamber.

rim-fire: A cartridge that has its primer located inside the rim of the case. See also **cartridge.**

rod: A rod used for cleaning a firearm. It is used to check for obstructions prior to loading the firearm. It may also be referred to as a ramrod, proving stick or dummy rod.

round: One shot fired by a firearm. It is also a complete item of ammunition or a cartridge that has all the components needed to fire one shot.

round-nose bullet: A bullet with a rounded nose.

S

sabot: A plastic sleeve that holds a slug that is smaller than the bore diameter of a firearm. It is used mainly in shotguns and muzzleloading firearms.

safety: A device that blocks the firing mechanism of a firearm.

scope: See **sight.**

sear: Part of the firing mechanism linked to the trigger. The sear holds the hammer, firing pin or striker in the cocked position until the trigger is squeezed.

secure locking device: See under Appendix D: Legal Definitions.

semi-automatic:
a) An action which fires, extracts, ejects, chambers and cocks with each separate pull of the trigger.
b) For registration purposes, a repeating firearm requiring that the trigger be pulled for each shot fired and which uses the energy of the discharge to perform part of the operating cycle; sometimes called auto-loading or self-loading actions.

semi-wad cutter: A cylindrical bullet with a short-truncated cone at the nose. Often used for paper target shooting.

shell: A complete unit of ammunition consisting of a hull, primer, powder, wad and projectile(s) for use in shotguns.

shotgun: A shoulder firearm with a smooth bore designed to fire multiple pellets called shot, or a single projectile called a slug.

shot shell: A cartridge used in a shotgun. It contains multiple-shot pellets or a single projectile called a slug.

side by side: A firearm, usually a shotgun, with two barrels placed side by side.

sight: A firearm device, either mechanical or optical, that helps the shooter aim accurately.

single action: An action that releases the hammer from a cocked position when the trigger is pulled. Usually found on handguns.

single action revolver: A revolver that requires the hammer to be cocked manually. Pressing the trigger will not cause it to fire until this is done.

single shot: For registration purposes, a single-barrel firearm that is manually loaded and has no magazine-feed device.

slide safety: A device that blocks the firing mechanism of a firearm.

sling: A strap used to carry and aid in aiming a rifle.

slug: A large single projectile used in shotguns. See also **rifled slug.**

small bore: Generally refers to a .22-calibre firearm or rim-fire ammunition.

smokeless powder: Propellant powder used in modern firearms.

smooth bore: A firearm with a bore that is not rifled, such as a shotgun.

soft-point bullet: A bullet with a partial jacket exposing a portion of the lead core at the nose.

spent bullet: A bullet near the end of its flight that has lost nearly all its energy. Despite a loss in energy, spent bullets can still penetrate targets.

spire-point bullet: A bullet with a cone-shaped nose.

stock: The part of a rifle or shotgun used in holding the firearm against the shoulder when firing.

T

tang safety: A device that blocks the firing mechanism of a firearm.

telescopic sight: See **sight.**

trajectory: The path a projectile takes during flight.

trigger: The part of the firearm mechanism that releases the part of the action that fires the cartridge.

trigger guard: The metal loop around the trigger made to protect it and prevent accidentally touching the trigger.

U

unattended: See under Appendix D: Legal Definitions.

unloaded: See under Appendix D: Legal Definitions.

V

vehicle: See under Appendix D: Legal Definitions.

velocity: The speed at which a projectile travels in a given direction.

W

wad: A paper fibre or plastic disc used to separate the powder charge from the shot or slug, to seal propellant gases behind the charge, and to hold the shot together in the barrel.

wad-cutter: A cylindrical bullet with a sharp-shouldered, nearly flat nose. It is designed to cut paper targets cleanly so they can be scored accurately.

wheel lock: An early firearm mechanism. A wheel with serrated edges is spun against a piece of iron pyrite. This sends sparks into the pan to ignite the charge.

wing safety: A device that blocks the firing mechanism of a firearm.

X

No applicable entry.

Y

No applicable entry.

Z

No applicable entry.